What's being said about MSP University?

"... (MSP University has) been on the cutting edge of the (MSP) movement and has helped many partners wade through the muddy waters. They continue to refine the process and share that information with their peers. We have gained much from our relationship with them and use their tools to continue growing our Managed Services practice."

- Arlin Sorensen, President/CEO, Heartland Technology Solutions, HTG Peer Groups, Iowa

"...I probably never would have been able to come up with a deal this creative if it wasn't for everything MSPU has taught me! You are totally changing the way I look at opportunities."

- Mark Sanders, President, AJMaddox Technologies, Texas

"...I am currently in the process of transitioning from a professional services model to a managed services provider here in south OC so that I can build up my company's client base and get more recurring revenue. These resources have proven to be very valuable in directing me towards my goals."

- Neil Richards, President, TotalTech Inc., California

"...MSPU has become the premier training house for managed services....."

- Karl Palachuk, Founder, KPEnterprises, Great Little Book, SMBBooks, California

What's being said about The Guide to a Successful Managed Services Practice?

"This book sits on my shelf and my service manager's shelf. You can't get $99 worth of consulting this valuable. It's a great reference, a great start, and worth looking at for everyone looking at managed services."

- Dave Sobel, President, Evolve Technologies, Virginia

"Every Small Business consultant needs to read this book. Yes, it's an awesome guide to managed services. But it's also a great guide to deciding which services to sell, how to price them, how to sell them, and how to "deliver" after you've inked the deal.

Did you need to know how to run a help desk? Or how to create an escalation procedure? It's all here.

You'll save literally hundreds -- maybe thousands of hours of work by reading this book. I run a very successful managed services business and I learned a great deal from this book. Simpson deserves a big hand for putting together such a valuable guide."

- Karl W. Palachuk, Founder, KP Enterprises, California

"...a "must-have" for any organization considering offering proactive, flat-rate I.T. Services"

"Packed with lots of valuable tools and other information that would have likely taken years to acquire on our own."

- Kurt Sippel, President, Applied Tech Solutions, Wisconsin

"This book was instrumental to getting our Managed Services practice to increase by about 2 1/2 times in less than 18 months. And I'm talking about a five figure number, too! The fundamental steps really work if you'll just stick to the plan outlined in the book. I recommend it to all my peers."

- Frances G. Miller, CEO, Dynamic Computer Solutions, Kansas

"What you don't know you don't know is in this book. Do yourself (and your clients) a favor, read this book and put to practice what you learn. I had to rethink the way I historically ran my business after reading (this) book and I am impressed with the results from the changes that I have made. My contracts, pricing structure, and how I handled different types of work were all reviewed and altered as a result of knowledge gained from this book.

You will be money and time ahead and proud that you invested such a small financial amount in your business and reaped so much in return."

- Travis B. Creighton, President, Computron, Florida

"This book provides the real world information and tools you need to understand and implement Managed Services in your company. The authors have obviously LIVED the transition from break fix to recurring revenue streams, and have provided a roadmap to success for others looking to make the same transition."

- Gavin Steiner, President, Interprom Inc., Canada

What's being said about The Best I.T. Sales & Marketing BOOK EVER!?

"The title to this book says it all. It really is the Best IT Sales and Marketing book ever. NUFF SAID!!!! YOU NEED TO BUY THIS BOOK if you want to turn your IT Business into a profitable one. I can't wait for (MSPU's) next book; hopefully (they) won't keep us waiting too long :-)"

- Chris Timm, Managing Director, TCG Computer Services, England, UK

"For those that have no formal marketing plan in place for their business this book is the how-to cookbook that will make it simple for you to be a great marketer. The tried and true approaches in this book are many of the tactics we use in our business. It is also laid out simply so that you don't need a marketing background to be able to understand and take action on the advice."

- Dan Hay, President/CEO, isoutsource.com, Washington

"This book is jam-packed with valuable insight to assist IT VAR's in selling and marketing to Small Business. It is required reading for my company's sales and marketing staff. I highly recommend it to anyone whether new to the business or an old veteran."

- Philip Kenealy, President, ACES, Iowa

If you want to grow a consistent services business, buy this book and start marketing now. You will recoup several times this book's cost with your first marketing campaign

- Mark Saum, President, Fidelis, TX

MSP University's

Managed Services Series

The Best NOC and Service Desk Operations BOOK EVER!

For Managed Services...

Erick Simpson
MCP, SBSC

MSP University
7077 Orangewood Avenue, Suite 104
Garden Grove, CA 92841
www.mspu.us

Voice: (855) 772-6778

Fax: (866) 230-0649

Printed in the United States of America

ISBN 978-0-9788943-3-7

Library of Congress Control Number: 2009912497

Library of Congress subject heading:

Computer Consulting
Information Technology Management
Information Technology Service

Contents

The Best NOC and Service Desk Operations BOOK EVER!

Table of Contents

The Best NOC and Service Desk Operations BOOK EVER!

Table of Contents

The Best NOC and Service Desk Operations BOOK EVER!

Table of Contents

The Best NOC and Service Desk Operations BOOK EVER!

Table of Contents

The Best NOC and Service Desk Operations BOOK EVER!

Table of Contents

The Best NOC and Service Desk Operations BOOK EVER!

Table of Contents

The Best NOC and Service Desk Operations BOOK EVER!

Table of Contents

The Best NOC and Service Desk Operations BOOK EVER!

Table of Contents

The Best NOC and Service Desk Operations BOOK EVER!

Table of Contents

The Best NOC and Service Desk Operations BOOK EVER!

Table of Contents

The Best NOC and Service Desk Operations BOOK EVER!

Table of Contents

As always, every form, tool and piece of collateral discussed in this book is available as a download after registration at: www.mspu.us/nocbookregistration.

About the Author – Erick Simpson

As Co-founder, Vice President and CIO of Intelligent Enterprise and MSP University, Erick Simpson has experienced first-hand the challenges of growing an I.T. business. Intelligent Enterprise provided Information technology solutions to the Southern California SMB market for 11 years, beginning in 1997. Their relationships with partners such as Microsoft, Cisco, Citrix and HP allowed them the ability to design, scale and implement effective infrastructure solutions for their diverse client base.

Intelligent Enterprise, a Microsoft Gold Certified and Business Solutions partner and Small Business Specialist, became one of the first "pure-play" MSPs in the SMB space, and successfully migrated to a managed services business model in January of 2005. Prior to this, they were operating as many other I.T. providers have – reacting to clients in "break-fix" mode, and dealing with the constant demand to recruit new clients and sell new solutions each and every month in order to meet their receivables goals.

Intelligent Enterprise developed an "all you can eat" managed services approach focused on 3 core deliverables – remote help desk, proactive network monitoring, and they pioneered vendor management. Through the creation of a managed services sales and marketing approach unique to the industry, Intelligent Enterprise sold over $2MM worth of managed services agreements before being asked to share their managed services knowledge and expertise through their managed services university at www.mspu.us.

MSP University has helped numerous manufacturer, vendor, distributor and franchise membership organizations, their channels, and thousands of independent IT service organizations worldwide educate themselves in transitioning IT service businesses to successful, profitable managed services practices through its educational, training, fulfillment and consulting services.

A recognized IT and Managed Services author, speaker and trainer, and contributor to numerous industry publications and events, Erick is the author of "The Guide to a Successful Managed Services Practice - *What Every SMB IT Service Provider Should Know...*", the definitive book on Managed Services, and the follow-ups in MSP University's Managed Service Series; "The Best I.T. Sales & Marketing BOOK EVER!", focused on helping I.T. and managed services providers grow their businesses through effective passive and direct marketing techniques proven to win business and increase revenues, and "The Best I.T. Service Delivery BOOK EVER!", written to help service providers deliver hardware warranty, break-fix, professional services and managed services efficiently and profitably; as well as illustrating effective migration strategies for moving from one service delivery model to another, affording the ability to create additional revenue streams.

Erick's professional certifications include Microsoft MCP and SBSC. Erick has conducted nationwide managed services workshops, boot camps and presentations at industry events such as the Microsoft Worldwide Partner Conference, CompTIA Breakaway, SMBNation, SMBSummit, ITPro Conference, ITAlliance, ICCA, MSPRevolution, Ingram Micro Seismic Partner Conference, ConnectWise Summit, Kaseya Connect, Autotask Community Live!, WatchGuard Partner Conference, HTG All Conference and others, as well as numerous industry user group meetings.

Erick also co-authored Arlin Sorensen's HTG Peer Group publication *"Peer Power – Powerful Ideas for Partners from Peers "*, available at www.htgmembers.com, and his recent articles on managed services are available at the following web urls:

The Importance of the Sales Engineer in Growing an IT Services Practice – Author, Enterprise Management Quarterly May 2009 - http://www.emqus.com/index.php?/emq/article/the_importance_of_the_sales_engineer_in_growing_an_it_services_practice_994

Winning Business in a Losing Economy – Author, Channelpro April 2009 - http://www.channelprosmb.com/article/2027/Winning-Business-in-a-Losing-Economy

Managed Services FAQ Guide – Author, SearchITChannel September 2008 - http://searchitchannel.techtarget.com/guide/faq/0,296293,sid96_gci1332072,00.html#

Maximize Service Delivery Profits During Economic Downturns – Author, MSPMentor July 2008 - http://www.mspmentor.net/wp-content/uploads/2008/06/maximizing-service-delivery-profits-during-economic-downturnsdoc.pdf

We Can't Just Sell Managed Services – Author, MSPMentor June 2008 - http://www.mspmentor.net/wp-content/uploads/2008/06/we-can-t-just-sell-managed-servicesdoc.pdf

About the Author – Erick Simpson

The Importance of Vertical-Specific Marketing for MSP's – Author, Focus On MSP May 2008 -
http://www.focusonmsp.com/articles/20080415-3.aspx

Managed Services, your business plan and you – Author, SearchITChannel July 2007 -
http://searchitchannel.techtarget.com/general/0,295582,sid9 6_gci1262243,00.html

Managed Services – What's All the Buzz About? Author, Microsoft Small Business Channel Community -
https://partner.microsoft.com/us/40029753

Managed Services – It Makes Sense – Author, ChannelPro June 2007 –
http://www.channelpro-digital.com/channelpro/200706/?folio=38

An Introduction To Managed Services – Author, Infotech Update January 2007 –
http://infotech.aicpa.org/NR/rdonlyres/AC23261D-D7F4-4459-A822-DFD4FDA8F999/0/it_jan_feb07.pdf

Erick lives in Orange County, California with his wife Susan and their two sons, Connor and Riley. His prior technical experience includes overseeing the design, development and implementation of Enterprise-level help desks and call centers for Fortune 1000 organizations.

About the Author – Erick Simpson

Visit Erick's blog at: http://blog.mspu.us.

Dedication

To my wife Sue and our sons Connor and Riley I lovingly dedicate this book. Without your constant support and understanding I wouldn't be able to do what I love to do.

Acknowledgements

There are so many people who have influenced, encouraged and continue to inspire us to succeed, and I'd like to personally thank them here.

I'd again like to thank my business partner of so many great years of ups and downs, challenges and successes, Gary Beechum. It's rare to find a business partner and best friend with whom you can have a relationship longer than many marriages! We're a great team – each of us balances the other's weaknesses and strengths to a point where we strike a natural balance, and are much more effective together than we would ever be apart. Thanks, Gary – it really does keep on getting better and better.

Special thanks to Mark Sanders, our amazing Webmaster, for putting up with us over the last several years and supporting every crazy last minute request, no matter what time of day or night it is – Mark, thanks for everything you've done to help us continue to achieve greater levels of success.

I'd like to recognize our excellent, dedicated staff for all the hard work they constantly put in to keep our organization moving forward; Quinn Nguyen, Tanisha Jefferson, Noelle Bannon, Nilo Nogueras, Jerry Moran, Valerie Cano, Matt Dow,

The Best NOC and Service Desk Operations BOOK EVER!

Acknowledgements

Kate Hunt, Ly Lai, Adrian Cue, Rafael Sanguily, Andrew Baduria, Cesar Ordaz, Christina Tang, Giovanni Sanguily, Maryanne Garcia, Mo Guerrero and Jasmine Cano – we couldn't do it without you.

Foreword

Thank you for purchasing the newest publication. Being the fourth book in our Managed Services Series, with the first (The Guide to a Successful Managed Services Practice) covering an overview of managed services, the second (The Best I.T. Sales & Marketing BOOK EVER!) covering sales and marketing and the third (The Best I.T. Service Delivery BOOK EVER!) covering building, growing and maximizing a service delivery practice, this book covers the next logical area in an MSP's business – NOC and Service Desk operations.

Coming from enterprise IT, my background in building, staffing, training and managing Service Desks and call centers has served us well in both our MSP practice (which we sold in 2007) and in our current role as educators, mentors and fulfillment partners for our MSP University members worldwide.

As I sat down to develop the outline of this book, I could not help but be reminded of the fact that no matter how large or small the service organization, basic best practices processes and procedures for NOC and Service Desk operation are universal.

The Best NOC and Service Desk Operations BOOK EVER!

Foreword

Our relationships with our members have brought to light just how beneficial a structured incident management and service delivery process can be in increasing service delivery efficiencies (read profits) and client satisfaction. The more you standardize your processes and procedures, and train and enforce accountability among your technical resources to adhere to them, the more consistent your clients' experience. And this consistency is the key to client satisfaction – *as long as the outcomes are favorable!*

The goal of this book is to provide you with a set of these best practices processes and procedures to help improve your NOC's and/or Service Desk's performance and eliminate pain and risk for both you and your clients.

Let's get started...

Preface

It's hard to believe that another year has come and gone since the release of our last book, "The Best I.T. Service Delivery BOOK EVER!". It really does feel like we are all moving at "Internet Speed" these days – and it seems tougher and tougher to stay abreast of all of the changes in the industry and business climate we have all experienced in the past year.

Let's see...the biggest single issue we have seen affecting the industry and the service providers supporting it has been the economy. I'm sorry to report that as the bad economy has forced many businesses to close their doors, the ripple effect has caused many of these business' vendors to also disappear – including service providers. And this outcome has not only affected the small provider – we have seen a number of large service organizations also fold as a result of being highly leveraged and not reacting quickly enough to economic stressors.

Many service providers have survived; however, through a combination of cost-cutting and efficiency improvement measures – becoming leaner and meaner and working with their existing clients to come up with creative payment arrangements and discounts for them in an effort to show solidarity and loyalty. This "we're all in this together" approach has met with more positive results than negative, and has created stronger partnerships between many providers and their clients.

The same approach has been taken in reverse with distributors, manufacturers, vendors and financial institutions by savvy service providers who have worked out more favorable terms with them on their lines of credit and finance rates.

Another item to note in the past year is the increased competition among vendors serving the MSP space – especially in their pricing models. We now have a wide variety of PSA, RMM, NOC and Service Desk vendors with very competitively priced deliverables, with many including "pay as you go" pricing options. This makes it much more affordable for aspiring, as well as established MSPs to benefit from these services – and specifically from outsourced NOC and Service Desk vendors. This opportunity has helped some service providers survive and even thrive during the recession, and assisted others in reducing their overall costs and increasing their efficiencies by adopting their outsourced vendors' incident management and escalation processes, tools and training. As a result, we dedicate a section of this book specifically to outsourcing components of your NOC and

Service Desk when it makes sense, and how to integrate and manage these relationships.

Social media and communities round out my top three "game changers" for 2009. I strongly encourage you to watch the short "**Social Media Revolution**" video uploaded to YouTube at http://www.youtube.com/watch?v=sIFYPQjYhv8 for a reality check on where your prospects are heading and how you will need to modify your communications, marketing and sales strategies in order to remain competitive in the era of social media.

Communities are where your prospects will congregate in the future. The **Online Social Graph**, described by Clara Shih in her excellent book "The Facebook Era", as *"the World Wide Web of people – a map being constructed by social networking sites, such as Facebook, LikedIn and Hoover's Connect, of every person on the Internet and how they are interlinked"*, is where agile, forward-thinking organizations see a tremendous amount of marketing opportunity – both for new leads and for existing client interaction and retention. In fact, these communities are seen as such powerful new ways to cultivate relationships that MSP University will be integrating one into our online presence in 2010, which will include the capability for our members to create blogs, participate in forums and job boards, submit questions and rate responses and build virtual relationships with each other.

But we are not alone in this regard – both Autotask and ConnectWise, two of the leading PSA vendors in the industry, already have a head start with their communities, and CompTIA; a member-driven, non-profit industry trade association, will be launching communities of their own in 2010. And most of the industry's vendors and their clients are beating paths to create pages, groups and communities in popular social networking sites like Facebook, LinkedIn, Twitter and more.

These are just a few of the "game changers" of 2009 – it will be interesting to see what 2010 will offer, with economic recovery looming around the corner and the additional opportunities it will bring, as well as new industry game changers such as the cloud, SaaS and the concept of "free" being leveraged by organizations like Google to dominate search, online advertising, social networking and beyond...

As always, every form, tool and piece of collateral discussed in this book is available as a download after registration at: www.mspu.us/nocbookregistration.

Introduction

If you are new to MSP University's Managed Services series, welcome! Our goal in continuing to release publications centered on IT business transformation and improvement is to provide you a series of industry best practices honed by experience to help you reduce your operational costs, improve your efficiencies, increase your sales and raise the value of each sale. If you can make incremental, continual positive change in each of these four areas of your practice, the overall increase in your net profits over time will be considerable.

If you are already familiar with our Managed Services series, then you have come to know and appreciate the way in which we deliver our content. Rather than approach these concepts via a high-level theoretical discussion, we prefer the direct approach of a "boots on the ground", step-by-step methodology which illustrates the strategic reasons behind the best practices we espouse as well as the tactical activity required to execute them. Based on feedback from our readers, this approach is appreciated, as it allows our books to become more than interesting diversions for their organizations, instead becoming more akin to operations manuals for specific departments, and making the required reading lists for many businesses.

In fact, if you have ever attended one of our Boot Camps, you will recall being required to read and complete comprehension tests for several of our books as a requirement for your attendance. This allows us to bring all of our attendees to a baseline understanding of our general philosophies regarding eight areas of successful IT service practice operations:

1. Leadership
2. Financial Benchmarking
3. Organizational Structure
4. Talent Management
5. Marketing
6. Sales
7. Service Delivery
8. Vendor Relationships

Once these basics are understood by our Boot Camp attendees, we are much more effective in providing the diagnostic and prescriptive training, mentoring and support they need in improving these critical areas of their businesses.

If you are interested in attending one of our Boot Camps, please browse to www.mspu.us/bootcamps for more information and our international schedule.

What Can You Expect From This Book?

Among the topics we will explore in this publication are best practices for building, maintaining and maximizing the efficiencies and effectiveness of your NOC and Service Desk operations. This means that our discussion will include the people, processes and systems required to operate a best-in-class NOC and Service Desk.

This book is broken down into logical sections to support the creation of your NOC and Service Desk, beginning with considerations for infrastructure design, hardware, services and the tools and technology to power your deliverables; which is the next area we will explore, along with your supported hardware, applications, services and vendors.

We will discuss your service agreements and SLAs, along with your NOC and Service Desk's tiering structures, incident and problem management procedures and escalation processes to maintain these SLA's.

We will also dive deeply into people – including your staff; your clients and their staff, and your and your clients' vendors. For the section on your staff, we will discuss effective hiring, training, compensating, incenting and managing your talent to reward performance that improves your bottom line. Elsewhere, we will explore how best to interact and communicate with your clients and their vendors, and set and manage your clients' expectations, as well as how to get the most out of your own vendor relationships.

We will also explore basic client requirements necessary for you to support them, and their environments' minimum standards for service, as well as essential pre- and post-sales activities required for successful on-boarding, provisioning , service go-live and ongoing support and maintenance.

Next, we will concentrate on identifying the key performance metrics and indicators that will be used to baseline your existing NOC and Service Desk's performance and profitability. These same KPIs will be used to measure improvement in specific areas over time as you implement the methodologies contained in this resource.

Finally we will explore the topic of outsourcing some or all of your NOC and Service Desk operations to third-party resources, and what you should consider when determining your strategy in this area. If and when you decide to implement an outsourcing strategy, our discussion will cover integration strategies with your existing processes, how to effectively transition your clients and successfully manage all of your outsourced relationships in order to maintain and increase client satisfaction over time, and scale your services more broadly with less internal staff.

The Difference Between a NOC and a Service Desk

The role of a NOC and Service Desk is to manage and maintain availability of services for their end users or clients and to facilitate the restoration of normal service operation while minimizing impact to these end users or clients within an agreed-upon SLA. In this capacity the NOC and Service Desk may provide the following services to the end user or client according to their SLA:

- Incident Management
- Problem Management
- Configuration Management
- Change Management
- Risk Management
- Release Management
- Service Level Management
- Availability Management
- Capacity Management
- IT Service Continuity Management
- Security Management
- Communication Management

The Difference Between a NOC and a Service Desk

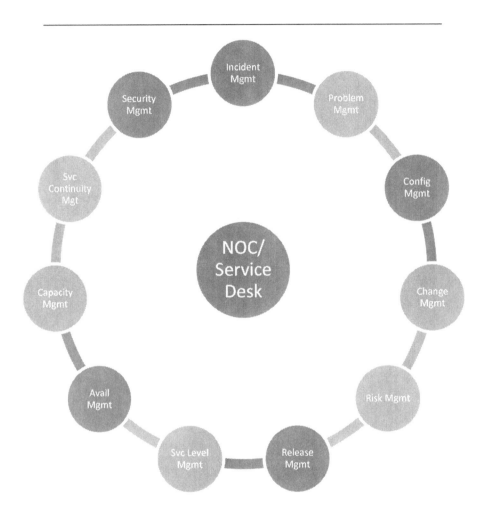

Figure 1 – NOC and Service Desk Roles

The day-to-day duties of the NOC and Service Desk include:

- Receiving all incident notifications and service requests
- Recording all incidents and service requests
- Classifying all incidents and service requests

- Prioritizing all incidents and service requests
- Troubleshooting all incidents and service requests
- Escalating all incidents and service requests as necessary to maintain SLAs
- Maintaining consistent communication with all parties affected by the incident or service request
- Performing all scheduled maintenance activities

Although many of the roles, processes, procedures, activities and responsibilities of a NOC and a Service Desk and their respective personnel are more alike than they are dissimilar, there is one important differentiator between these two business units: *their focus*.

In its most literal form, a NOC's duties and responsibilities are oriented towards proactively managing and maintaining efficient operating states of hardware devices, software operating systems and applications and insuring the continuity of services; and responding to incidents and problems that impact these. This definition most naturally lends itself to conducting activities such as remote monitoring and patch and change management for devices, software and services, and which *do not normally require direct interaction with end users*.

In contrast, a Service Desk's and its staff's duties and responsibilities are focused on *managing end user incidents and problems*. In fact, the Service Desk is the single point of contact (SPOC) for all end user issues, which are identified,

---

documented, prioritized and assigned to internal resources for troubleshooting and resolution prior to the performance of quality assurance activities and final closure.

However; this does not imply that these two business units do not interact with each other, or that the NOC never communicates with an end user. Exceptions do exist here, as in any situation, and issues can be escalated freely between these units during maintenance and incident and problem management activity.

In addition, depending upon specific factors, there does not need to be an official "NOC" or "Service Desk" at all – as long as the service provider's staff delivers these functions by following best practices processes and procedures to maintain their SLAs and satisfaction with their clients, this may be perfectly acceptable.

Let's explore this thought further...if we may not need an official "NOC", or "Service Desk", would we need dedicated NOC and Service Desk staff? In some cases, and specifically for smaller service providers – we may not. Again – as long as there exist resources to perform or manage these functions, these hats may be interchangeable.

It is completely feasible and realistic to have resources perform both NOC and Service Desk functions during the normal course of service delivery. The challenge over time with this becomes the efficient and effective scaling of capacity as the service provider's client base grows. There will come a tipping point where it makes sense for the service provider to dedicate specific resources to particular job functions, or outsource some of these functions in order to scale, increase efficiencies and maintain client satisfaction.

It is also a common practice among smaller service organizations for individual resources to conduct all incident and problem management activities through several levels of escalation. What this means is that a resource may continue to work a specific issue as it makes its way from Tier 1 through Tier 2 escalations and beyond, based upon the client's SLA and the NOC's or Service Desk's corresponding tiering and escalation procedures. Again, there may come a tipping point in the evolution of the service provider's business where it makes sense to dedicate specific resources to individual tiers, but this may be a long time coming, since industry statistics reflect that *ninety percent of all end user service requests are closed in Tier 1*, with an additional seven percent in Tier 2 and the balance in Tier 3.

This means that dedicating specific resources to tiers beyond Tier 1 must be justified by the sheer number of Tier 2 and Tier 3 requests being received by the Service Desk, and explains why the dedication of specific resources to each of these tiers is more readily found in enterprise-level corporate service desks, or industry manufacturer, vendor and distributor support offerings.

Section 1: Infrastructure Design

The outsourced service provider or internal service manager in the enterprise will need to insure that their infrastructure meets the minimum requirements necessary to deliver effective and efficient NOC and Service Desk services within their SLAs. While some deliverables will have their own unique infrastructure requirements, in most cases, all services will generally share common requirements at both the provider's and clients' or end users' locations.

This section will explore these minimum requirements in areas of environmental, systems, communication and connectivity requirements.

Service Location Requirements - Provider

At the Provider's Location

Whether the location for delivering NOC and Service Desk services is a remote outsourced service provider's location, geographically displaced corporate branch office or the third floor in your corporate building, the basic infrastructure requirements needed to deliver these services effectively are identical, and will normally include the following:

- Environmental requirements
    - NOC/Service Desk
    - Data Center
- System requirements
    - Hardware
    - Operating systems and software
    - Services
- Communication requirements
    - Protocols
    - Security
- Connectivity requirements
    - Broadband
    - Remote access
- Business Continuity
    - Backup/DR Plan
    - Service Availability

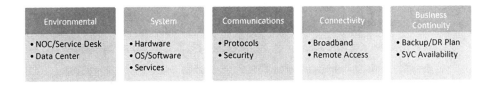

Figure 2 – Service Delivery Requirements at the Provider's Location

Environmental Requirements

NOC/Service Desk

The outsourced service provider or internal service manager will normally conduct NOC and Service Desk operations from a centralized location staffed with support personnel. The capacity planning, design, implementation and staffing of this facility for the effective delivery of these services require careful consideration for not only its current service delivery requirements, but future growth. Therefore, the business-critical functions and requirements of the facility necessitate the following:

- Physical security
- Adequate physical space planning, allowing for future growth
- Scalable, highly available redundant network infrastructure

- Continuous, redundant fail-over power
- Highly available, redundant voice and broadband carrier services
- Climate control
- Backup, disaster recovery and business continuity plan

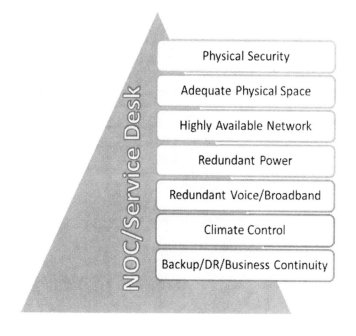

Figure 3 – Infrastructure requirements at the provider's location

NOC and Service Desk System Requirements

System requirements for NOC and Service Desk service delivery are defined as those minimum hardware, services, operating system and software applications, and configurations and patch and update levels necessary for proper system, services and application operation and efficient service delivery. Depending upon the specific deliverable and its associated SLA, these requirements may vary widely between outsourced service providers and internal service managers.

NOC and Service Desk Hardware Requirements

NOC and Service Desk hardware devices and components will need to meet certain minimum requirements to support their roles throughout the NOC and Service Desk service delivery lifecycle. Hardware housed at the outsourced service provider's or the internal service manager's NOC and Service Desk must meet certain physical requirements to fulfill its role in the service delivery process, and these may consist of the following:

- A specific CPU type and speed
- A minimum amount of physical RAM
- A specific amount of free HDD space
- A specific BIOS type and level
- Specific physical connectivity types
- Specific local and remote connectivity methods
- Supported protocols and ports
- Security methods
- Specific configuration
- Specific WAN/LAN/DMZ Location
- Interoperability with other local or remote devices
- Hardware redundancy

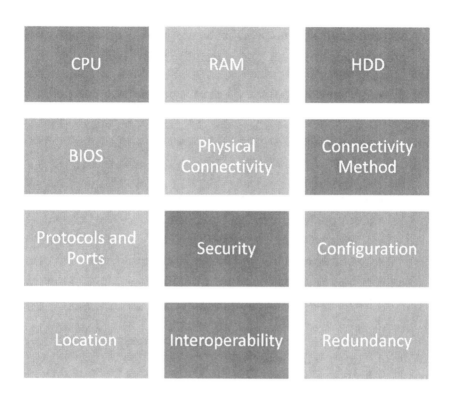

Figure 4 – Hardware requirements at the provider's location

NOC and Service Desk Operating Systems and Software Requirements

Just as there are minimum requirements for hardware housed at the outsourced service provider's or internal service manager's NOC and Service Desk to properly support its role during NOC and Service Desk service delivery, the same is true for operating systems and software, which must also meet certain requirements to fulfill its role in the service delivery process, and these may consist of the following:

- A specific operating system type, version and patch level
- A specific software application type, version and patch level
- Specific configuration
- Local and remote connectivity methods
- Supported protocols and ports
- Security methods
- Interoperability and ability to communicate with other local or remote systems, services, functions, databases and applications
- Service availability and redundancy
- Data backup, restoration and business continuity role and requirement

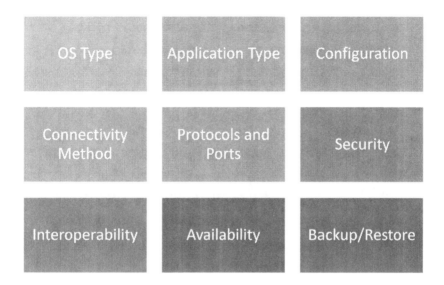

Figure 5 – Operating system and software requirements at the provider's location

Communication Requirements

Communication requirements for NOC and Service Desk service delivery are defined as those data and voice network, bandwidth and protocol requirements necessary to receive and aggregate performance data and alerts from managed locations; as well as deliver remote management and maintenance to endpoints at these locations. This remote management and maintenance can occur securely over wide area data networks, while communications and updates by and between the outsourced service provider's or internal

---

service manager's NOC and Service Desk and the end user or client can be delivered over these same data or voice networks. Robust remote monitoring and management, trouble ticketing and phone systems are required to provide minimum required communications capabilities in order to deliver NOC and Service Desk services efficiently.

Utilizing unified communications and next-generation call center solutions providing the ability to record all interactions with end users or clients, vendors and 3rd party support personnel allow valuable call accounting, monitoring and customer service benefits to the NOC and Service Desk.

Protocols

Protocols utilized by the outsourced service provider's or the internal service manager's NOC's remote monitoring and management solutions to collect performance data and alerts for events, services and applications include:

- Windows Management Instrumentation (WMI)
- Simple Network Management Protocol (SNMP)
- Syslog
- Network Basic Input/Output System (NetBIOS)
- Internet Control Message Protocol (ICMP)
- Extensible Markup Language (XML)

Security Requirements

Transmission of the aggregated performance data and alerts generated within disparate end user or client networks from remote monitoring and management solutions to the outsourced service provider's or the internal service manager's NOC and/or Datacenter is normally accomplished through secure protocols, and may include:

- Virtual Private Networks (VPNs)
- Secure Sockets Layer (SSL)
- Transport Layer Security (TLS)
- Hypertext Transfer Protocol over Secure Socket Layer (HTTPS)
- Secure File Transfer Protocol (SFTP)

Connectivity Requirements

In this context, connectivity requirements for NOC and Service Desk service delivery are defined as those services, devices and processes that allow the transfer of performance data and alerts from the remote monitoring and management solution at the end user's or client's location to the outsourced service provider's or the internal service manager's NOC and/or Datacenter, and provide remote access, control and desktop sharing capabilities to the outsourced service provider or the internal service manager and include network connections, equipment and services such as:

- Bridges

- Routers
- Switches
- Gateways
- Firewalls
- Broadband services
- Secure network protocols

Broadband Requirements

In order for successful delivery of NOC and Service Desk services, fast, reliable broadband carrier service at both the end users or client's location and the outsourced service provider's or the internal service manager's NOC and Service Desk are required to support both remote monitoring and management services from disparate end user or client networks, as well as to provide effective remote access capabilities for efficient maintenance services.

Remote Access and Control Requirements

The capability to remotely access endpoints in end user or client networks to share desktops and deliver NOC and Service Desk services is the cornerstone of a successful remote management and maintenance deliverable. By delivering services remotely, the outsourced service provider or internal service manager increases response and resolution times and is able to support more clients. Remote access to client networks can be facilitated via many remote monitoring and management tools and numerous 3rd-party software solutions as well as through:

- Virtual Private Networks (VPNs)
- Hypertext Transfer Protocol over Secure Socket Layer (HTTPS)
- Secure File Transfer Protocol (SFTP)
- Secure Telnet /Secure Shell (SSH)
- Microsoft Windows Terminal Services
- Microsoft Windows Remote Desktop Protocol (RDP)
- 3rd-party remote control solutions

Disaster Preparedness and Business Continuity Requirements

In order to insure the high availability of Service Desk and NOC operations, the outsourced service provider or the internal service manager must develop and implement strategies to insure business continuity in the event of service interruption or disaster. This Business Continuity Plan must assume a worst case scenario of total inaccessibility to the Service Desk or NOC and initially provide all of the recovery steps necessary to support the Service Desk and NOC's critical business functions.

Based upon the severity and extent of the service interruption or disaster, the plan must also provide for the timely restoration of other less critical business functions over time.

The plan must account for people, communications, hardware, operating systems and line of business applications, data, services, facilities to operate from and security.

In order to create the Business Continuity Plan, the outsourced service provider or internal service manager must determine the following:

1. Scope
   a. Areas to be covered by the Business Continuity Plan
2. Objectives
   a. What results are expected, and courses of action the Business Continuity team will follow
3. Assumptions
   a. What is taken for granted and assumed to be true

During the Business Continuity Plan requirements phase, the outsourced service provider or internal service manager must conduct a Business Impact Analysis to identify those business departments, functions, processes and systems that are most vulnerable to threat and are the most time-sensitive functions of the NOC and Service Desk.

The results of this analysis will help the outsourced service provider or internal service manager properly prioritize and schedule the recovery of interrupted NOC and Service Desk systems, communications, data, processes and functions.

Once this has been determined, a Recovery Coordinator and Recovery Team Leaders can be appointed, who will manage overall and specific operational unit Business Continuity Plan activities during an interruption or disaster. The next step in Business Continuity Plan development is to document the workflows for each business unit in addition to the NOC and Service Desk affected by the disruption such as IT, HR, sales, etc., to utilize as a roadmap in their re-creation when necessary. These units, along with their recovery/restoration processes will differ depending upon whether the disruption is experienced by the outsourced service provider or internal service manager.

All systems and applications must be identified and documented in the Business Continuity Plan as well as vital records and the absolute minimum requirements for NOC and Service Desk Operation to continue.

Next the outsourced service provider or internal service manager must identify if alternate means of operation currently exist, perhaps through hosted solutions in the cloud that can be accessed from other locations, for instance. Primary and secondary application support personnel contacts and vendors need to be identified next. Finally, how business units will function during recovery and the resources necessary for recovery will need to be documented by prioritized time frame.

The goal of the Business Continuity Plan is to allow the outsourced service provider or internal service manager the ability to quickly restore NOC and Service Desk functionality in the event of disruption, and is a necessary requirement in order to maintain agreed-upon SLAs for end users and clients. This section barely skims the surface of this complex topic.

Service Location Requirements - Datacenter

At the Provider's Datacenter

Because data centers are designed as highly secure, disaster-hardened facilities with backup and redundant power, data communications and environmental controls, they are judged to be the best solution to insure business continuity for equipment housed and services hosted there. The Datacenter is the facility used by the outsourced service provider or the internal service manager to house data and voice hardware such as servers, routers, switches, firewalls, gateways and communications equipment, as well as operating systems and software applications critical to maintaining highly-available services and effective service delivery processes to end users or clients. Due to the high costs associated with building and operating a Datacenter, many service providers and enterprise service managers lease space in existing 3rd-party Datacenters to avail themselves of these facilities and their services at a significantly reduced initial cost. Requirements of a Datacenter include:

- Physical security
- Scalable, redundant network infrastructure
- Redundant environmental controls
- Continuous, redundant distributed power
- Fire detection and prevention systems
- Redundant voice and broadband carrier services

- Backup, disaster recovery and business continuity plan

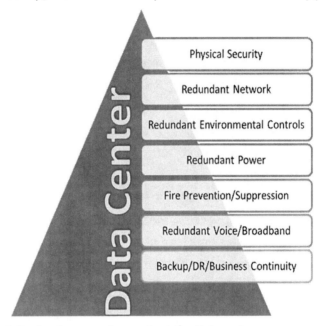

Figure 6 – Infrastructure requirements at the Datacenter

Datacenter System Requirements

Datacenter system requirements for NOC and Service Desk service delivery are defined as those minimum hardware, services, operating system and software applications, and configurations and patch and update levels necessary for proper hosted system, services and application operation and efficient hosted service delivery. Depending upon the specific deliverable and its associated SLA, these requirements may vary widely between outsourced service providers and internal service managers.

Datacenter Hardware Requirements

Datacenter hardware devices and components will need to meet certain minimum requirements to support their roles throughout the NOC and Service Desk service delivery lifecycle. Highly available hardware housed at the outsourced service provider's or the internal service manager's Datacenter must meet certain physical requirements including:

- A specific CPU type and speed
- A minimum amount of physical RAM
- A specific amount of free HDD space
- A specific BIOS type and level
- Specific physical connectivity types
- Specific local and remote connectivity methods
- Supported protocols and ports
- Security methods
- Specific configuration
- Specific WAN/LAN/DMZ Location
- Interoperability with other local or remote devices
- Hardware redundancy

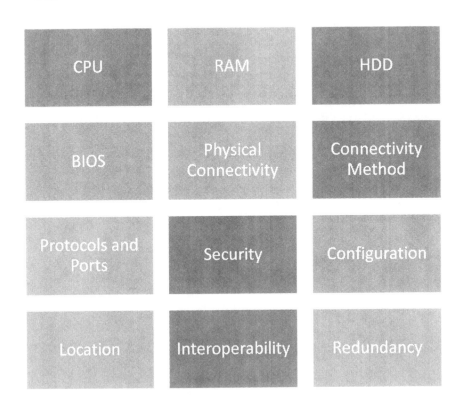

Figure 7 – Hardware requirements at the Datacenter

Datacenter Operating Systems and Software Requirements

Just as there are minimum requirements for hardware housed at the outsourced service provider's or internal service manager's Datacenter to properly support its role during NOC and Service Desk service delivery, the same is true for operating systems and software, any of which may be hosted at the Datacenter, whose specific requirements may consist of the following:

- A specific operating system type, version and patch level
- A specific software application type, version and patch level
- Specific configuration
- Local and remote connectivity methods
- Supported protocols and ports
- Security methods
- Interoperability and ability to communicate with other local or remote systems, services, functions, databases and applications
- Service availability and redundancy
- Data backup, restoration and business continuity role and requirement

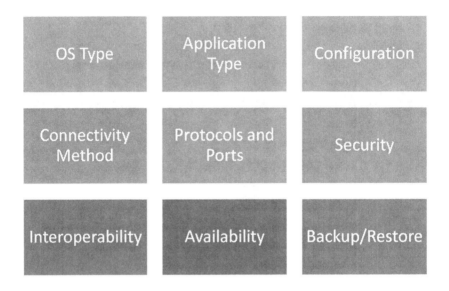

Figure 8 – Operating system and software requirements at the Datacenter

Datacenter Communication Requirements

In this scenario, communication requirements for an outsourced service provider or internal service manager's Datacenter to support NOC and Service Desk service delivery are defined as those network, bandwidth and protocol requirements necessary to support the receipt, transmittal and aggregation of performance data and alerts from and between managed locations, the Datacenter and the NOC and Service Desk; as well as to support delivery of remote management and maintenance to Datacenter and end user and client endpoints.

Datacenter Security Requirements

Transmission of data between the outsourced service provider's or internal service manager's Datacenter, NOC and Service Desk is normally accomplished through secure protocols, and may include:

- Virtual Private Networks (VPNs)
- Secure Sockets Layer (SSL)
- Transport Layer Security (TLS)
- Hypertext Transfer Protocol over Secure Socket Layer (HTTPS)
- Secure File Transfer Protocol (SFTP)

In addition, hardened physical security measures governing entrance to and egress from the Datacenter and access to the outsourced service provider's or internal service manager's equipment and their and their end user's or client's data must be implemented, monitored and managed.

Datacenter Connectivity Requirements

In this context, Datacenter connectivity requirements for NOC and Service Desk service delivery are defined as those services, devices and processes that allow connectivity and communications from the Datacenter to managed end user or client locations and the outsourced service provider's or the internal service manager's NOC and Service Desk, and provide remote access, management and control of the hosted devices, operating systems, software applications and services to the outsourced service provider or the internal service manager and include redundant network connectivity, equipment and services such as:

- Bridges
- Routers
- Switches
- Gateways
- Firewalls
- Broadband services
- Secure network protocols

Service Location Requirements – Outsourced 3rd Party Provider's Location

At the Outsourced 3rd Party Provider

More and more 3rd party back-office NOC and Service Desk providers are entering the market with offerings that either improve the outsourced service provider's or internal service manager's existing NOC and Service Desk operations, supplant portions of their deliverables or replace them completely.

These outsourcers provide private-labeled NOC and Service Desk services to IT service providers as well as corporate IT departments and assume the roles of these departments on a contract basis; delivering services as the IT service provider or corporate IT department so well that end users or clients may not be aware of the outsourced relationship between the parties.

Should the outsourced service provider or internal service manager choose to engage with one or more of these outsourced 3rd party providers, they would be wise to understand these outsourcers' existing infrastructure designs in areas including environmental, systems, communications and connectivity in order to evaluate their suitability in maintaining the outsourced service provider's or internal service manager's downstream SLAs to their end users or clients.

Service Location Requirements – Outsourced 3rd Party Provider

These infrastructure requirements should closely align with those maintained by the outsourced service provider or internal service manager in areas of redundancy, availability, communications, connectivity and business continuity:

- Environmental requirements
  - o NOC/Service Desk
  - o Data Center
- System requirements
  - o Hardware
  - o Operating systems and software
  - o Services
- Communication requirements
  - o Protocols
  - o Security
- Connectivity requirements
  - o Broadband
  - o Remote access
- Business Continuity
  - o Backup/DR Plan
  - o SVC Availability

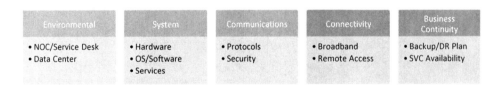

Figure 9 – Service Delivery Requirements at the Outsourced 3rd-Party Provider's Location

Additional requirements to consider when engaging with a 3rd party outsourced NOC or Service Desk are discussed in Section 8 – Outsourcing NOC and Service Desk Components.

Service Location Requirements – End User/Client

At the End User's or Client's Location

Infrastructure requirements needed at the end user's or client's location for successful NOC and Service Desk service delivery will normally include the following:

- Environmental requirements
  - Customer location
- System requirements
  - Hardware
  - Operating systems and software
  - Services
- Communication requirements
  - Protocols
  - Security
- Connectivity requirements
  - Broadband
  - Remote access

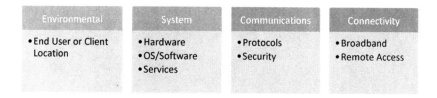

Figure 10 – Service Delivery Requirements at the End Client's Location

---

Environmental Requirements

Client Location

The outsourced service provider or internal service manager will normally install remote monitoring and management agents on individual, dedicated or shared hardware at the end user's or client's location as required by their chosen RMM (remote monitoring and management) solution. Therefore, the business-critical functions of these solutions necessitate the following environmental requirements at these locations:

- Physical security of the dedicated or shared host hardware
- Continuous, redundant power
- Highly available voice and broadband carrier services
- Secure redundant means of remote as well as physical access
- Climate control
- Backup, Disaster Recovery and Business Continuity Plan for outsourced provider's or internal service manager's remote monitoring and management hardware

Service Location Requirements – End User/Client

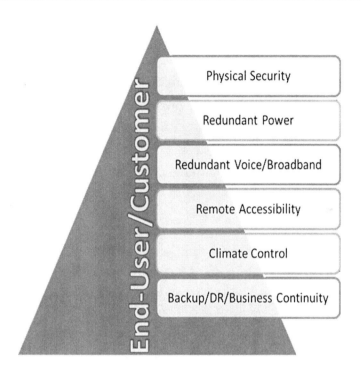

Figure 11 – Environmental Requirements at End User or Client Location

System Requirements

System requirements for NOC and Service Desk service delivery are defined as those minimum hardware, services, operating system and software applications, configurations and patch and update levels necessary for proper system and application operation to allow the effective delivery of services. Depending upon the specific deliverable and its associated SLA, these requirements may vary widely between outsourced service providers and internal service managers.

Hardware Requirements

Hardware devices and components at the end user's or client's location will need to meet certain minimum requirements as dictated by the outsourced service provider or internal service manager's RMM solution. Based upon its specific function and application in the service delivery process, physical requirements of the hardware may include the following:

- A specific CPU type and speed
- A minimum amount of physical RAM
- A specific amount of free HDD space
- A specific BIOS type and level
- Specific physical connectivity types
- Specific local and remote connectivity methods
- Supported protocols and ports
- Physical security
- Specific configuration
- Specific WAN/LAN/DMZ Location
- Interoperability with other local or remote devices
- Hardware redundancy

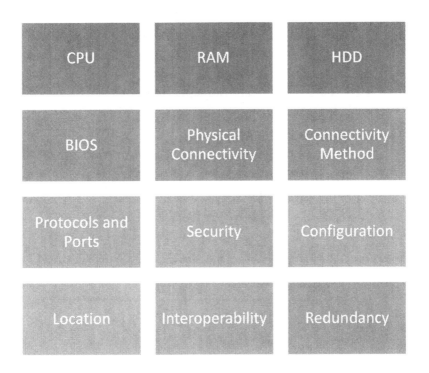

Figure 12 – Hardware Requirements at End User or Client Location

Operating Systems and Software Requirements

Just as there are minimum requirements for hardware to properly support its role during NOC and Service Desk service delivery, operating systems and software running on hardware at the end user's or client's location must also meet specific criteria, and these requirements may consist of the following:

- A specific operating system type, version and patch level

- A specific Software application type, version and patch level
- Specific configuration
- Local and remote connectivity methods
- Supported protocols and ports
- Security methods
- Interoperability and ability to communicate with other local or remote systems, services, functions, databases and applications
- Service availability and redundancy
- Data backup, restore and business continuity process

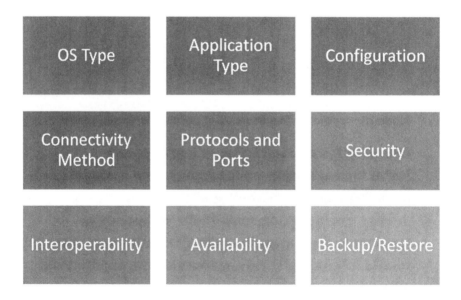

Figure 13 – Operating System and Software Requirements at End User or Client Location

Communication Requirements

Communication requirements for NOC and Service Desk service delivery are defined as those network and protocol requirements necessary to receive and aggregate performance data and alerts from end user and client locations, as well as to allow delivery of remote management and maintenance to endpoints at these locations. This remote management and maintenance can occur securely over wide area data networks, while communications and updates from the outsourced service provider or internal service manager to the end user or client can be delivered over either data or voice networks.

Protocols

Protocols utilized by remote monitoring and management solutions to collect performance data and alerts for events, services and applications include:

- Windows Management Instrumentation (WMI)
- Simple Network Management Protocol (SNMP)
- Syslog
- Network Basic Input/Output System (NetBIOS)
- Internet Control Message Protocol (ICMP)
- Extensible Markup Language (XML)

Security Requirements

Transmission of the aggregated performance data and alerts generated within disparate end user or client networks from remote monitoring and management solutions to the outsourced service provider's or the internal service manager's NOC and/or Datacenter is normally accomplished through secure protocols, and may include:

- Virtual Private Networks (VPNs)
- Secure Sockets Layer (SSL)
- Transport Layer Security (TLS)
- Hypertext Transfer Protocol over Secure Socket Layer (HTTPS)
- Secure File Transfer Protocol (SFTP)

Connectivity Requirements

In this context, connectivity requirements for NOC and Service Desk service delivery are defined as those services, devices and processes that allow the transfer of performance data and alerts from the remote monitoring and management solution at the end user's or client's location to the outsourced service provider's or the internal service manager's NOC and/or Datacenter, and provide remote access, control and desktop sharing capabilities to the outsourced service provider or the internal service manager and include network connections, equipment and services such as:

- Bridges
- Routers
- Switches
- Gateways

- Firewalls
- Broadband services
- Secure network protocols

Broadband Requirements

In order for successful delivery of NOC and Service Desk services, fast, reliable broadband carrier service at the end users or client's location is required to support both remote monitoring and management services from disparate end user or client networks, as well as to provide effective remote access capabilities for efficient maintenance services by the outsourced service provider or internal service manager.

Remote Access and Control Requirements

The capability to remotely access endpoints in end user or client networks to share desktops and deliver NOC and Service Desk services is the cornerstone of a successful remote management and maintenance deliverable. By delivering services remotely, the outsourced service provider or internal service manager increases response and resolution times and is able to support more clients. Remote access to client networks can be facilitated via many remote monitoring and management tools and numerous 3rd-party software solutions as well as through:

- Virtual Private Networks (VPNs)
- Hypertext Transfer Protocol over Secure Socket Layer (HTTPS)

- Secure File Transfer Protocol (SFTP)
- Secure Telnet /Secure Shell (SSH)
- Microsoft Windows Terminal Services
- Microsoft Windows Remote Desktop Protocol (RDP)

Backup, Disaster Preparedness and Business Continuity Requirements

In order to insure the high availability of Service Desk and NOC operations, the outsourced service provider or the internal service manager must develop and implement strategies to insure the rapid restoration of dedicated remote monitoring and management hardware in the event of failure.

Basic requirements include having a backup of the remote monitoring and management device hardware's configuration and a replacement on hand, as well as the ability to replace the physical device to maintain established SLAs.

Section 2: NOC and Service Desk Tools and Technology

For purposes of our discussion, we will focus on four key tools for outsourced service providers and internal service managers to consider in powering their NOC and Service Desks:

- A remote monitoring and management (RMM) solution
- A trouble-ticketing or Professional Services Automation (PSA) Solution
- A remote access or control solution
- A Voice communications solution

Choosing and implementing the appropriate tools will help the outsourced service provider or internal service manager reduce costs through standardization and increased efficiencies and improve end user or client satisfaction by delivering proactive maintenance and consistent, auditable service delivery. The right tools will help realize these outcomes for the following reasons:

- In order to maximize net profits, outsourced service providers and internal service managers must develop and implement effective policies and procedures to improve their efficiencies in service delivery, and look to these tools as a starting point, leveraging their built-in templates, workflows and functionality

- In order to standardize and document incident and problem management and resolution, outsourced service providers and internal service managers use their tools' Service Desk functionality to improve and document their service delivery activity to end users and clients

- In order to show value to the end user or client, outsourced service providers and internal service managers rely on their tools' abilities to generate meaningful reports which can be utilized not only for service validation but; for the outsourced service provider, also to identify revenue-generating opportunities, such as when a device or service's monitored threshold is consistently exceeded, signaling an upgrade or up-sell opportunity

- In order to be alerted as quickly as possible to potential problems in end user or client environments, outsourced service providers and internal service managers establish proactive alerting and escalation of alerts in order to maximize their response time, providing them the ability to respond proactively to prevent or minimize service interruption

- In order to speed response and resolution times, outsourced service providers and internal service managers leverage these tools to remotely access and control end user or client devices, desktops and laptops

- In order to improve staff utilization, outsourced service providers and internal service managers schedule and automate the delivery of common maintenance activities such as operating system, application software, antivirus and antispyware patching and updating through the use of these tools, freeing their staff to work on higher priority or greater revenue-generating activities

- By administering maintenance and end user support services remotely, outsourced service providers and internal service managers further increase their efficiencies and staff utilization, and improve end user or client response and resolution time, raising client satisfaction

- By providing unified messaging, CRM integration, custom call routing, recording and accounting capabilities, next generation voice communications solutions improve the service delivery experience and increase satisfaction for end users and clients

Figure 14 – NOC and Service Desk Tool Benefits

Remote Monitoring and Management Tools

The Remote Monitoring and Management Tool

The ability for the outsourced service provider or internal service manager to proactively monitor critical devices and services is a fundamental necessity for the capability to maintain and increase service uptime. The most effective network monitoring solutions allow the outsourced service provider or internal service manager to install a software agent on individual, dedicated or shared hardware devices such as a server or desktop in a client's environment and initially obtain data on network-connected devices such as:

- Hardware asset, role and inventory information
- Operating system, application software and licensing and patch level information
- Device IP addressing information
- Physical system information (memory, disk, NIC, etc.)
- Running processes
- Up/down device status

After a predetermined period of time, the remote monitoring and management tool will be able to gather data and report on items such as the following:

- Syslogs
- Event Logs
- System Uptime

While all real-time network monitoring tools share some commonality, others provide more granular, meaningful reporting and alerting on equipment, such as:

- Output a topological map of the environment
- Detailed inventory to the module level
- Real-time and historical CPU, memory and interface statistics
- VPN monitoring
- VoIP application monitoring
- Voice trunk and DSP utilization
- The ability to back up and restore specific device configurations
- Equipment end-of-life and end-of-sale monitoring

Remote Monitoring and Management Tools

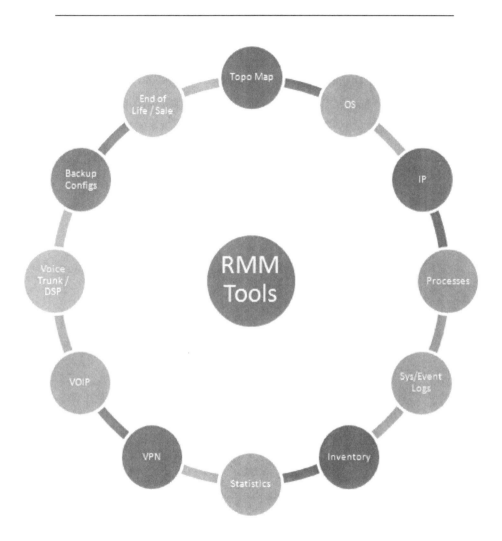

Figure 15 – Remote Monitoring and Management Tool Benefits

Remote Monitoring and Management Tools

The remote monitoring and management tool's capability to allow the outsourced service provider or internal service manager to configure pre-set alert thresholds for critical devices and services is a key to maximizing service uptime for end users or clients and maintaining SLAs. Commonly monitored devices and services include:

- Servers
- Routers
- Switches
- Firewalls
- IP Phones
- Access Points
- PCs
- Printers

In addition to hardware devices, critical services can also be monitored, alerted on and escalated. Commonly monitored services include:

- Broadband Services
- Email Services
- Web Services
- SQL Services
- Backup Services
- Antivirus Services

- VPNs
- Bandwidth
- VoIP QOS

Not only hardware and services can be monitored, but critical line-of-business applications are also capable of being monitored and alerted on. Remote monitoring and management tools normally utilize the following protocols to perform their function:

- WMI
- Syslog
- SNMP

Many remote monitoring and management tools integrate with numerous manufacturers' SNMP Management Information Bases (MIB) for their network hardware, providing the ability to quickly identify devices, operating systems and software applications and begin monitoring and managing them with ready-made templates containing the manufacturers' recommended operating thresholds. The outsourced service provider or internal service manager can configure the remote monitoring and management tool to trigger alerts when these thresholds are reached, as well as modify the alerts to trigger upon reaching customized operating thresholds.

Another added benefit to many remote monitoring and management tools is their ability to perform scheduled, scripted actions such as delivering patches and updates to operating systems and software applications and conducting device optimization operations such as disk defragmentation, deletion of temporary files and more for servers, desktops and laptops. For many of these tools, if an activity can be scripted, it can be scheduled to run unattended during off-hours, providing the outsourced service provider or internal service manager tremendous labor savings by offloading these mundane, time-consuming and labor-intensive activities from their costly human resources to their remote monitoring and management tool.

In addition, the ability to automatically restart failed services can also be configured in many of these remote monitoring and management tools, speeding restoration of critical services and minimizing downtime – all without human intervention. And along with alerts, all activity conducted by these tools is captured and available for reporting, creating an audit trail that can be reviewed at any time, further reducing the need to manually remote in to end user or client environments to ascertain whether patches were deployed successfully or backup jobs ran without error.

What to look for in a Remote Monitoring and Management Tool

The outsourced service provider or internal service manager today has the benefit of a wide variety of Remote Monitoring and Management tools to choose from, and several factors will weigh in their final purchase decision, including:

- Suitability for their particular service delivery model, needs and supported hardware and services
- Cost and ROI
- Implementation, training and deployment time
- The ability to provide meaningful reporting
- The quality of vendor support
- The ability to, and ease of integration with, their trouble ticketing or Professional Services Automation solution

The outsourced service provider or internal service manager whose service delivery model focuses on supporting Microsoft operating systems and software and IBM-compatible hardware benefit from the widest selection of remote monitoring and management tools. Those whose service delivery models include support for operating systems such as Apple, Linux, Unix and Novell, and other 3rd-party software and hardware will find their choices for remote monitoring and management tools more limited.

Many remote monitoring and management tool vendors include hosted, or "pay as you go" pricing models, lowering the barrier to entry for the outsourced service provider or internal service manager, as well as other, more traditional pricing models. Hosted remote monitoring and management tool solutions also reduce implementation and deployment time, as the need for the outsourced service provider or internal service manager to procure, build and configure host server hardware is eliminated.

The ability for the remote monitoring and management tool to document alerts, errors and informational data through a robust reporting engine is necessary when validating the outsourced service provider's or internal service manager's services to end users or clients, and crucial when justifying budget requests for service or equipment upgrades and during capacity planning.

As a result of remote monitoring and management tool vendors' efforts to gain market share, overall vendor support has improved, with services such as sales and marketing training, templates and collateral being offered, in addition to product training. Outsourced service providers and internal service managers should make certain to choose a vendor that provides support during their hours of service delivery. Depending upon the vendor and outsourced service provider's or internal service manager's geographic locations, time zone factors should be considered.

A critical function that the remote monitoring and management tool must provide is tight integration with the outsourced service provider's or internal service manager's trouble ticketing or Professional Services Automation solution. The remote monitoring and management tool must be able to communicate alerts to the trouble ticketing or Professional Services Automation solution and open a service request, documenting the alert, and enabling the trouble ticketing or Professional Services Automation solution to assign the appropriate priority and SLA to the service request, and escalate the incident as appropriate.

RMM Tool Generates Alert   Alert Forwarded To PSA Solution   PSA Solution Opens Service Request, Prioritizes and Escalates

Figure 16 – Remote Monitoring and Management and PSA Tool Integration Example

---

Trouble Ticketing and Professional Services Automation Tools

The Trouble Ticketing and Professional Services Automation Tool

Choosing and implementing a Service Desk Trouble Ticketing system in the outsourced service provider's or internal service manager's NOC and Service Desk is the next step in improving efficiencies by enabling the implementation of consistent, measurable workflow processes and reporting capabilities across these business units.

On the most fundamental level, basic Service Desk Trouble Ticketing systems may include the following capabilities:

- A service request or trouble ticketing component
- A scheduling & dispatching component
- A time tracking component
- A configuration & change management component
- A knowledge base component
- A resource management component
- A reporting component

For some outsourced service providers and many internal service managers these Trouble Ticketing systems' basic capabilities may be sufficient to meet their service delivery needs. Should the outsourced service provider or internal service manager require additional capabilities including tight integration with Remote Monitoring and Management tools and consolidated reporting between their Remote Monitoring and Management and Service Desk activities, a Professional Services Automation solution might be a better choice.

Effective Professional Services Automation solutions provide added benefits over basic Trouble Ticketing systems, and these benefits may include:

- A CRM system
- A service request or trouble ticketing component
- A project management component
- A scheduling & dispatching component
- A time tracking component
- An expense tracking component
- An inventory control component
- An asset management component
- A configuration & change management component
- A service agreement & SLA management component
- A knowledge base component
- A resource management component
- Quoting & invoicing integration with accounting systems
- A sales funnel component
- A marketing campaign management component

- Tight two-way integration with many Remote Monitoring and Management tools through APIs
- Robust, customizable consolidated reporting
- Community and user group interaction and support

In addition, a Professional Services Automation solution improves efficiencies by implementing consistent workflow processes and communication and reporting capabilities across multiple business units which may include:

- Service Desk
- NOC
- Professional Services
- Marketing
- Sales
- Purchasing
- Inventory
- Accounting

As a Professional Services Automation solution not only supports but extends the capabilities of traditional Trouble Ticketing systems, moving forward we will focus on and reference Professional Services Automation solutions as they pertain specifically to our NOC and Service Desk-focused discussions.

The Professional Services Automation solution's CRM functionality allows the outsourced service provider or internal service manager the ability to automate their NOC and Service Desk's workflows and record and report on end user or client-facing processes such as sales, marketing, projects and other services. Applied correctly, this process-based mechanism helps maintain SLAs, boosts client satisfaction, shortens sales cycles, simplifies incident and project management, facilitates escalation and improves problem identification and resolution time.

Other NOC and Service Desk functions benefiting from a Professional Services Automation solution include effective resource management through efficient scheduling and dispatching, time tracking and expense management – with key metrics including utilization and profitability by resource, deliverable and end user or client easily tracked and reported on.

The ability for the Professional Services Automation solution to manage end user or client assets and configurations further increases the outsourced service provider's or internal service manager's efficiencies and speeds problem resolution. And, when paired with change management, the outsourced service provider or internal service manager can insure that standardized methods and procedures are followed to handle

---

all changes to an end user's or client's infrastructure, minimizing the negative impact of any change-related activity.

In order to effectively deliver incident management and resolution services, the outsourced service provider or internal service manager will leverage the Professional Services Automation solution's service request, or trouble ticketing component, and build their NOC and Service Desk deliverables around an effective, standards-based incident management process; incorporating incident identification, prioritization and escalation for timely resolution – all governed by strict SLAs.

The ability for the outsourced service provider's or internal service manager's Remote Monitoring and Management tool to integrate with the Professional Services Automation solution's service request component is critical for maximizing efficiencies and maintaining SLAs, as alerts are passed from the Remote Monitoring and Management tool to the Professional Services Automation solution to automate the creation, prioritization and escalation of service requests. As incidents are closed, the Professional Services Automation solution updates its internal searchable knowledge base with each resolution, allowing the outsourced service provider's or internal service manager's staff the ability to quickly query their own internal database during future incident management activity - a true benefit, especially when dealing with specific line-of-business applications or unique hardware and software configurations.

Integration with an outsourced service provider's or internal service manager's quoting and accounting solutions further extends the value of the Professional Services Automation solution, reducing redundant data entry, increasing efficiencies and speeding turnaround time for end user or client quotes and invoices.

The outsourced service provider's or internal service manager's ancillary processes also benefit from the Professional Services Automation solution's ability to create customized workflows based upon specific solution sales processes and cycles, tracking each milestone during the sales process and managing the sales funnel as applicable. As with the service request component, the sales component enforces a strict sales process, standardizing each step in the sales cycle and providing meaningful data through reporting, which allows the outsourced service provider or internal service manager to forecast potential revenue accurately, or modify sales processes in order to achieve their desired outcome.

In many cases, implementing a Professional Services Automation solution into an outsourced service provider's practice or internal service manager's operation and enforcing management of each business unit by the processes and workflows established will be difficult and challenging; however, in order to transition to not only a proactive service delivery model, but also a proactive business operations model, it may be the most efficient and effective answer.

Figure 17 – Professional Services Automation Solution Benefits

---

What to look for in a Professional Services Automation Solution

As in an outsourced service provider's or internal service manager's decision to purchase a Remote Monitoring and Management tool, similar factors weigh in the Professional Services Automation solution's purchase decision:

- Suitability for the outsourced service provider's or internal service manager's particular service delivery model
- Cost and ROI
- Implementation, training and deployment time
- The ability to provide meaningful reporting
- The quality of vendor support
- The ability to, and ease of integration with, their Remote Monitoring and Management tool

Like many Remote Monitoring and Management tool vendors, many Professional Services Automation solution vendors also offer "pay as you go" pricing models, lowering the barrier to entry for outsourced service providers and internal service managers, as well as other, more traditional pricing models. And as with hosted Remote Monitoring and Management tools, hosted Professional Services Automation solutions also reduce implementation and deployment time.

Remote Access and Control Tools

The Remote Access and Control Tool
Another necessary tool in delivering effective NOC and Service Desk services is the outsourced service provider's or internal service manager's Remote Access and Control solution, or solutions, as there are two specific scenarios addressed by these tools:

- Remotely accessing equipment
- Remotely sharing a desktop session with an end user or client

These scenarios each require a different capability and approach by the Remote Access and Control solution. In the case of remotely accessing equipment, the outsourced service provider or internal service manager can use already-existing methods, such as Secure Telnet or SSH, or VPN with RDC for newer Microsoft Windows server and desktop operating systems. But in situations that require interaction with an end user or client remotely, the outsourced service provider's or internal service manager's Service Desk will need the ability to share the user's desktop, take control of the user's keyboard and mouse, and interact with them in real-time for effective and timely incident identification and resolution.

It is appropriate to note that many Remote Monitoring and Management tools have remote access and control capabilities built in for certain devices and operating systems.

What to look for in a Remote Access and Control Tool
An outsourced service provider or internal service manager today has the benefit of a wide variety of Remote Access and Control tools to choose from, and as with any purchasing decision of this type, factors that will weigh in their final decision include:

- Suitability for their particular service delivery model and supported hardware, operating systems, software applications and services
- Cost and ROI
- Implementation, training and deployment time
- The availability and quality of vendor support

Outsourced service providers or internal service managers whose service delivery models focus on supporting Microsoft operating systems and software, and IBM-compatible hardware benefit from the widest variety of Remote Access and Control tools. Those whose service delivery models include support for Apple, Linux, Unix or Novell operating systems will find their choices for Remote Access and Control tools much more limited.

As with Remote Monitoring and Management tools and Professional Services Automation solutions, many remote control tool vendors include hosted and "pay as you go" pricing models, as well as other, more traditional pricing models. Many of the Remote Access and Control tools available to the outsourced service provider or internal service manager are easy to implement, simple to deploy and do not require extensive training to utilize effectively. Effective Remote Access and Control Tools should provide the following functionality:

- Secure connectivity to the target device
- The ability to take complete control of the target device
- Fast performance
- The ability to perform file transfers between source and target devices
- The ability to print from the target device to the host device's printers
- The ability to switch focus between the target device to the source device, allowing the end user to view the source device's desktop (for training and other purposes)
- The ability to rapidly deploy, or make available any necessary Agents to the target device

- A Web-based architecture to allow functionality from any source device in any location

Any solution that allows access to an internal network should be secure, minimizing the end user's or client's external footprint. The Remote Access and Control tool should provide this security natively, in order to be considered a viable choice for the outsourced service provider or internal service manager, allowing the most flexible support options.

The ability to completely control the target device by the outsourced service provider or internal service manager's staff greatly increases their capacity to quickly and effectively troubleshoot end user or client issues remotely, increasing utilization, efficiency and client satisfaction.

The Remote Access and Control tool's performance is critical during remote incident resolution – the faster the response, the better for both the outsourced service provider or internal service manager and the end user or client.

The ability to transfer data between devices is also a requirement, as the replacement of operating system or software application files is a common necessity during incident troubleshooting and resolution, as is the deployment of patches and updates to the target device from time to time.

Printing files accessed from the target device to the source without the necessity to install and configure printer drivers also benefits the outsourced service provider or internal service manager's staff during incident resolution.

Rapid deployment of Remote Access and Control Agents, or the ability to host these Agents on the outsourced service provider or internal service manager's website or support portal provides maximum speed and availability for remote access and control support to the end user or client, and the ability to provide this support from any web browser at any location provides maximum flexibility in addressing end user or client issues.

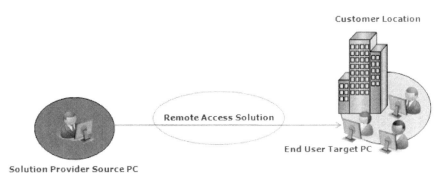

Figure 18 – Remote Access and Control Example

Voice Communications Solutions

The Voice Communications Solution

The outsourced service provider or internal service manager must equip their NOC and Service Desk with a robust voice communications solution in order to effectively deliver NOC and Service Desk services to their end users or clients. The availability and proper operation of this system is equally, if not more important, than any of the other tools and technologies employed by the outsourced service provider or internal service manager in the delivery of services.

For maximum benefit to the outsourced service provider or internal service manager and to improve satisfaction of their end users or clients, it is imperative for the NOC and Service Desk to:

- Reduce blockage (busy signals)
- Improve response time
- Increase first call resolution
- Shorten average call time
- Reduce queue hold times
- Shrink abandon rates

In order to facilitate these goals, the chosen voice communications solution should support the following minimum features:

- Scalability
- Automatic call distribution (ACD) or customizable call routing (CCR)
- Interactive voice response (IVR)
- Call monitoring
- Call recording
- Call accounting (Reporting)

Obviously, the ability to scale as the outsourced service provider's or internal service manager's NOC and Service Desk grows is important, as is automated call distribution, which allows calls to be routed based upon any number of criteria including resource availability, time of day, urgency, client, etc.

The interactive voice response capability of the voice communications solution allows the creation of intuitive menus to manage calls effectively and efficiently, and get the caller to the right queue for service through voice or keypad response to the auto attendant's voice prompts.

The ability to monitor and record interactions between end users or clients and NOC and Service Desk staff allows the outsourced service provider or internal service manager to insure quality of service, facilitate training and maintain a digital record that can be archived should the necessity arise to produce it at a later date.

The call accounting feature is also important in that it allows the outsourced service provider or internal service manager to analyze call volume and activity through any number of filters, including queue, resource, time of day, day of week, duration of call and more. This information is invaluable in staffing and scheduling activities – as well as identifying training needs.

Additional voice communications solution features that can further benefit the outsourced service provider's or internal service manager's NOC and Service Desk include:

- Unified communications capability
- VoIP support
- Integration with Professional Services Automation solutions

The ability to support unified communications will allow the outsourced service provider or internal service manager the most flexibility in managing and maintaining visibility to all inbound and outbound voice communications by providing an additional level of communications capability to their staff – especially in smaller organizations where staff responsibilities may take them away from the NOC or Service Desk.

VoIP integration provides benefits including the ability to use softphone software applications on desktops and laptops, allowing support to be delivered and calls managed anywhere an internet connection is available, in addition to enabling support delivery from geographically displaced locations or home offices simply by plugging in an inexpensive VoIP handset to a broadband connection and maintaining the same quality and level of support as if the resource were sitting in the NOC or at the Service Desk.

Finally, integration with the outsourced service provider's Professional Services Automation solution will enable advanced CRM functionality including screen pop-ups identifying the caller, their organization and other important information, as well as launching their company profile and logging the call, hopefully allowing the Service Desk to:

- Improve response time
- Increase first call resolution
- Shorten average call time

Figure 19 – Voice Communication Solution Goals

Integrating NOC and Service Desk Tools and Technologies

The Value of Integration

The more tightly integrated the outsourced service provider's or internal service managers' NOC and Service Desk tools and technologies are, the more effective they will be in scaling, maximizing service efficiencies, reducing costs, increasing client satisfaction and improving net profits.

In the same regard, failing to integrate these tools, along with their independent workflows and processes, will increase inefficiencies and prolong the time it takes to deliver services, requiring more manual labor-intensive activity to conduct NOC and Service Desk functions and consolidate reporting across disparate systems and solutions. This slows analysis of key performance metrics and indicators, negatively impacting overall operational oversight.

The obvious best answer for the outsourced service provider or internal service manager is so select a suite of solutions that can be integrated to deliver a superior set of benefits in combination than would otherwise be possible.

With this understanding, the outsourced service provider or internal service manager will utilize their Remote Monitoring and Management tools' and Professional Services Automation and Voice Communications solutions' integration capabilities to automate and reduce the manual labor necessary to manage automated alerts for monitored devices, operating systems, applications and services, as well as user-generated service requests as much as possible.

In addition to call recording and reporting benefits, when conducting any required voice communications with end users or clients, staff efficiencies and response times can be improved by utilizing "click to dial" functionality available through integration of the outsourced service provider's or internal service manager's Voice Communications solution and their Professional Services Automation's CRM module, alleviating the need to manually look up the correct contact numbers and physically dial them.

And when the necessity arises to conduct a remote access or control session during incident management, the ability to utilize the outsourced service provider's or internal service manager's Remote Monitoring and Management tool's built-in Remote Access and Control functionality speeds incident response and resolution times.

A potential outcome for this type of tight integration may resemble the following:

1. An alert is raised by the Remote Monitoring and Management tool based upon a monitored device

reporting an error or becoming unreachable, or as a result of a monitored service outage

2. The Remote Monitoring and Management tool opens a service request in the Professional Services Automation solution's Service Desk module and provides the granular data necessary for incident management and reporting to commence

3. The Professional Services Automation solution queries its internal database and appends additional key information to the service request such as information about the device and its configuration, the error, time of the alert, end user or client location and contact information and contract or SLA information and other necessary data to support incident management

4. Based upon the type of alert, the Professional Services Automation solution designates a priority to the service request, and an escalation process to maintain SLA, and assigns it to a support queue or a specific resource

5. The Professional Services Automation solution messages all affected parties of the nature of the alert and sets the end user's or client's expectations for incident management

6. The service request is addressed successfully by the outsourced service provider's or internal service manager's NOC or Service Desk staff; by utilizing their

---

Remote Monitoring and Management tool's Remote Access and Control function, and documenting their incident resolution activities, and the service request is eventually closed after appropriate QA activity is conducted

7. If the need to communicate directly with the affected end user or client is required, the integration between the Professional Services Automation solution's CRM component and the outsourced service provider's or internal service manager's Voice Communications solution can be leveraged through onscreen click-to-dial functionality, with call documenting, time-stamping and recording of each support call and appending it to the service request happening automatically

8. The Professional Services Automation solution communicates the resolution status of the service request to the Remote Monitoring and Management tool, which then cancels the alert

9. The outsourced service provider or internal service manager can now run consolidated reports and analytics against this and all incidents, aggregating data from the Remote Monitoring and Management tool and the Voice Communications and Professional Services Automation solutions

---

Integrating NOC and Service Desk Tools and Technologies

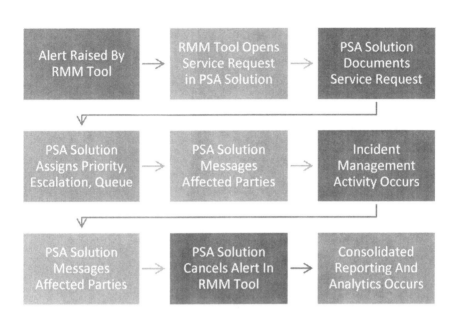

Figure 20 – NOC and Service Desk Tools and Technology Integration Supporting Incident Management and Reporting

Section 3: NOC and Service Desk Deliverables

In this section we will explore a NOC and Service Desk's deliverables, along with end user or client-facing requirements necessary for effective service delivery. These considerations include managing:

- Hardware
- Operating Systems
- Software Applications
- Services
- Users
- Locations
- Vendors
- Agreements/SLAs

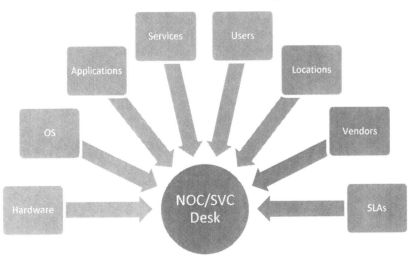

Figure 21 – NOC and Service Desk Focus

NOC Services

The NOC and Its Deliverables

In order to insure high availability of hardware, operating systems, software applications and services under management, the outsourced service provider's or internal service manager's NOC must continuously monitor their operating states and implement an alerting and response process to address incidents when these operating states deviate from established parameters.

In addition to continuously monitoring and reactively responding to alerts from managed endpoints and services, the NOC delivers proactive maintenance services such as patching and updating operating systems, software applications and device configurations, and optimizing the operational states of host devices and systems through activities such as deletion of temporary files, disk defragmentation, Active Directory, DNS, DHCP and Event Log management and pruning.

Remote Monitoring and Management

In order to maintain managed systems per service and maintenance agreements and their SLAs, the outsourced service provider or internal service manager must conduct continuous monitoring of these systems and services. This is facilitated through the Remote Monitoring and Management

---

tool's capabilities. There are specific actions that need to be carried out prior to official "turn up", or "go-live" of monitoring services for a new end user or client location.

These may include:

- Setting up the end user's or client's account in the Remote Monitoring and Management tool and Professional Services Automation solution
- If the Remote Monitoring and Management tool is appliance-based, configuring and deploying the appliance per manufacturer or vendor recommendations for secure communications to and from the end user or client location and the outsourced service provider's or internal service manager's NOC, Datacenter or Service Desk
- If the Remote Monitoring and Management tool is agent-based, configuring and deploying agents as required to monitor managed devices, operating systems, software applications and services per manufacturer or vendor recommendations and enabling secure Remote Access and Control and communications to and from the end user or client location and the outsourced service provider's or internal service manager's NOC, Datacenter or Service Desk

- If applicable, initializing a discovery routine by the Remote Monitoring and Management tool to identify all network-connected devices and their roles in the environment
- Associating the applicable Remote Monitoring and Management tool's default monitoring templates from its template library to all identified devices, operating systems, software applications and services
- Developing base monitoring templates and assigning them to all devices, operating systems, software applications and services which the Remote Monitoring and Management tool did not identify or does not have a default template for
- Testing and confirming proper two-way communications and alerting to and from managed devices, operating systems, software applications and services at the end user or client location and the outsourced service provider's or internal service manager's NOC, Datacenter or Service Desk
- Configuring, testing and confirming proper operation of the Remote Monitoring and Management tool's Remote Access and Control function for managed devices and operating systems
- Configuring, testing and confirming proper two-way integration with the Professional Service Automation Solution; with raised alerts resulting in properly

formatted service request generation including end user, device and client identification information, as well as correct status updating and alert cancellation occurring in the Remote Monitoring and Management tool upon service request resolution in the Professional Services Automation solution

- Configuring, testing and confirming proper scripting and deployment of unattended operating system and supported software application patches and updates
- Configuring, testing and confirming proper scripting and execution of unattended device and operating system optimization activities such as deletion of temporary files and disk defragmentation
- Configuring, testing and confirming proper report generation and automated report delivery
- Integrating Remote Monitoring and Management tool reporting into Professional Services Automation solution and testing
- Tweaking and tuning thresholds, alerting and reporting during an initial analysis period to insure outcomes meet expectations

Proactive Maintenance

Once the end user's or client's environment has been properly prepared to receive NOC services in this manner and based upon the associated SLA, the outsourced service provider or

---

internal service manager will create a proactive maintenance schedule for the managed devices, operating systems, software applications and services at the end user or client location. This schedule will govern the maintenance activities to be delivered by the NOC staff, and may include:

- Keeping operating system and software application service packs, patches and hotfixes current
- Optimizing operating systems, software applications, backups and hardware
- Rebooting servers and critical devices
- Installing software updates and upgrades
- Optimizing logical directory structures and keeping Active Directory Schemas and DNS configurations current

The outsourced service provider or internal service manager will leverage the Remote Monitoring and Management tool's ability to perform as much of this scheduled maintenance activity as possible during off-hours, report on outcomes and alert on failures, and provide the benefit of standardizing these activities across the end user or client base and freeing valuable human resources for other activities.

In addition to delivering scheduled maintenance activities, the NOC will review the Remote Monitoring and Management tool's monitoring reports daily to analyze the operating state of managed devices, operating systems, software applications and services to identify service degradation or potential failure in advance of its occurrence in order to take proactive preventative measures.

Reactive Response and Incident Management
The NOC will also respond to the Remote Monitoring and Management tool's alerts; indicating a device, operating system, software application or service is functioning outside of recommended parameters, and begin incident management activity reactively in these situations.

Some commonly monitored events by the NOC through the Remote Monitoring and Management tool may include:

- Backups
- Connectivity
- Cloud/Email/Web/SQL/FTP Services
- Windows Services/Events
- Device Memory Utilization/Performance
- Device Processor Utilization/Performance
- Device Hard Drive Utilization/Performance
- Router/Firewall Logs
- Antivirus Alerts
- Network Security/Unusual Traffic/Attacks
- VoIP QOS
- VPNs
- User Sessions/Authentication

Service Desk Services

The Service Desk and Its Deliverables

In order to insure high availability of end user's or client's information technology-supported business processes, activities and workflows, the outsourced service provider's or internal service manager's Service Desk must be equipped to address incidents when these processes, activities and workflows are degraded or interrupted.

Focused primarily on end user issues, the Service Desk functions as the single point of contact for end users or clients, and facilitates the restoration of normal service operation while minimizing impact to the user and delivering services within agreed-upon SLA's. In this capacity the Service Desk works directly with the end user or client, as well as with the NOC as needed to fulfill its responsibilities.

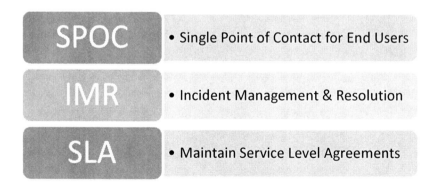

SPOC	• Single Point of Contact for End Users
IMR	• Incident Management & Resolution
SLA	• Maintain Service Level Agreements

Figure 22 – Service Desk Responsibilities

In order to achieve its objectives, the Service Desk will conduct the following end user or client-facing activities:

- **Receive all incident notifications** – this can be through any means established by the outsourced service provider or internal service manager - phone, fax, portal or email
- **Record all incidents** – this is accomplished through the Professional Services Automation solution's Service Desk component
- **Classify all incidents** – correctly document the nature of the incident, including affected users, systems, devices and services
- **Prioritize all incidents** – proper prioritization is essential to effective escalation
- **Route all incidents** – based upon factors such as classification and priority, the incident is assigned to the appropriate queue or resource for incident management and resolution
- **Troubleshoot all incidents** – perform established troubleshooting and incident management activity according to manufacturer's and vendor's best practices and outsourced service provider's or internal service manager's established procedures
- **Escalate all incidents as necessary** – proper internal and external escalation insures adherence to established SLAs, including escalation to 3rd-party vendors for support
- **Dispatch resources as needed** – if included in the end user's or client's agreement and SLA, the Service Desk

---

---

will perform dispatch functions and schedule onsite visits by internal or external physical resources including 3rd-party vendors per its established escalation process
- **Maintain consistent communication with all parties** – including end users, their managers and higher, onsite resources including 3rd-party vendors, and internal Service Desk management hierarchy
- **Perform all scheduled activities** – including but not limited to moves/adds/changes, maintenance, documentation and reporting

In order to maintain an effective Service Desk, internal objectives need to be clear, end user and client requirements and SLAs documented and understood; incident management, escalation and dispatch processes standardized and followed, and training for Service Desk staff as well as end users and clients needs to be conducted regularly. Service Desk deliverables need to be clearly defined and service levels monitored regularly and modified as needed. Additionally, clearly defined response, resolution and escalation times must be incorporated into an SLA and communicated to Service Desk staff as well as to end users and clients.

There are specific actions that need to be carried out prior to official "turn up", or "go-live" of Service Desk services for a new end user or client location.

These may include:

- Setting up the end user's or client's account in the Professional Services Automation solution and Remote Monitoring and Management tool
- Configuring, testing and confirming end user's or client's ability to generate properly formatted service requests with all required information via email and the Professional Services Automation solution's Service Desk portal
- After the Remote Monitoring and Management tool has been deployed and configured, testing and confirming the proper operation of its Remote Access and Control function for managed devices and operating systems
- Configuring, testing and confirming proper two-way integration with the Remote Monitoring and Management tool; with raised alerts resulting in properly formatted service request generation including end user, device and client identification information included, as well as correct status updating and alert cancellation occurring in the Remote Monitoring and Management tool upon service request resolution in the Professional Services Automation solution

---

- Integrating Remote Monitoring and Management tool reporting into Professional Services Automation solution and testing
- Configuring, testing and confirming proper report generation and automated report delivery

Vendor Management Services

The Value of Vendor Management

Vendor management is the process whereby the outsourced service provider's or internal service manager's NOC and Service Desk manages all interactions with the end user's or client's infrastructure vendors. This offloads that responsibility from the end user or client and allows them to focus on running their business. This service adds tremendous value to the relationship between the end user or client and the outsourced service provider or internal service manager; as no matter whether through an automatically-generated alert, or via the end user or client generating a service request directly, any incident requiring 3rd-party vendor support for issues affecting their infrastructure is managed by the NOC or Service Desk.

All vendor management activity, including activity conducted by infrastructure vendors during incident resolution, is documented in the Professional Services Automation solution by the NOC or Service Desk per the outsourced service provider's or internal service manager's standard incident management processes and procedures.

This service saves the end user or client the time and potential frustration of dealing with numerous vendors and also allows the outsourced service provider or internal service manager to proactively manage all infrastructure vendor activity. The NOC and Service Desk works with these vendors directly to either quickly resolve issues or schedule on-site vendor visits - both have been found to tremendously improve efficiencies and incident response and resolution times, hence improving client satisfaction.

End user or client infrastructure vendors that the outsourced services provider or internal service manager agree to manage may include:

- Telco/Long Distance/Teleconferencing vendors
- Broadband vendors
- Fax/Copier/Printer vendors
- Web/Application Development/Database vendors
- Line of Business Software vendors
- Hosting/Co-Location vendors
- Equipment vendors
- Point of Sale vendors
- Phone/VoIP System vendors
- Phone/VoIP Service vendors
- Cellular/Smartphone/PDA Service vendors
- Structured Cabling vendors

In order to provide Vendor Management services effectively, the outsourced service provider or internal service manager must provide all infrastructure vendors under management a Letter of Agency (LOA) signed by the end user or client, which grants them the authority to act on their behalf, allowing them the ability to open service requests and schedule maintenance and repair services as necessary.

Reporting

The Value of Reporting
The outsourced service provider or internal service manager will integrate the Remote Monitoring and Management tool's reporting function with the Voice Communication's and Professional Services Automation solution's to generate rich, customized consolidated reports for internal and external (or end user or client-facing) purposes.

The outsourced service provider or internal service manager will utilize specifically customized reports internally to analyze key metrics to evaluate NOC and Service Desk performance and modify internal processes and procedures to improve outcomes.

Externally, the outsourced service provider or internal service manager will utilize specifically customized reports with end users or clients to validate the successful delivery of services within SLA and according to existing service agreements; as well as to identify opportunities to improve the availability or performance of existing devices, operating systems, software applications and services through activities outside of the scope of the existing agreement or SLA. These activities may involve replacement or reconfiguration, which may or may not be conducted by the outsourced service provider or internal

---

service manager or their staff, but instead by an outside vendor or other provider.

Report areas commonly available through a Remote Monitoring and Management tool and Voice Communications and Professional Services Automation solutions may include:

- Device, operating system, software application and service performance reporting
- Device, operating system, software application and service maintenance reporting
- Alert and service request reporting
- Call-specific accounting reporting
- End user, client, NOC and Service Desk resource performance reporting
- SLA performance reporting
- Other customizable KPI reporting

When properly integrated and customized to provide meaningful data, these reports are a key tool utilized by the outsourced service provider or internal service manager to improve the NOC and Service Desk's performance and efficiencies, yielding greater net profits, as well as increasing end user or client satisfaction.

When creating end user or client-facing reports, it is a good idea to develop two versions – a very high-level executive

---

---

summary, and a more detailed report. In many cases, end users or clients will prefer the executive summary report over the detailed report. Always have the detailed report available when conducting strategic meetings with the end user or client, as you may wish to refer to it to dig deeper on specific topics during the conversation.

When developing your executive summary report template, make certain to include as many visual elements to represent the data as possible. The more charts, graphs and visual elements and less text, the better.

What Should a NOC and Service Desk Support?

Support Considerations

While an internal service manager and their NOC and Service Desk staff; whose responsibilities are to support an internal corporate IT infrastructure, may have little or no influence on establishing minimum requirements for the devices, operating systems, software applications and services they maintain in order to receive services, outsourced service providers may be more fortunate.

Whenever possible, the outsourced service provider or internal service manager should strive to establish and maintain minimum standards for service qualification. This helps standardize on hardware, operating systems, software applications and services, allowing the outsourced service provider or internal service manager to require their NOC and Service Desk staff to maintain proficiencies, skill sets and certifications on a controlled number of supported items, rather than a growing, ever-changing variety of systems and services. The benefits of this philosophy should be obvious, and include:

- More efficient and effective maintenance and incident resolution
- Faster on-boarding of new end users or clients

What Should a NOC and Service Desk Support?

- Speedier training and knowledge transfer by and between new and existing NOC and Service Desk staff
- Easier end user or client infrastructure setup and configuration of Remote Monitoring and Management tools and Professional Services Automation solutions
- Standardized performance metrics and reporting

As a result of these and other benefits, end user or client satisfaction is increased, and the outsourced service provider's or internal service manager's and their NOC and Service Desk staff's jobs are made much easier.

Some minimum standards required for an outsourced service provider or internal service manager's NOC and Service Desk to provide services for hardware, operating systems, software applications and services at end user or client locations may include:

- Specific vendor-supported server, desktop and laptop hardware and BIOS versions
- Specific vendor-supported routers, access points, switches and firewalls
- Specific vendor-supported voice hardware and BIOS versions
- Specific vendor-supported cellular, Smartphone and PDA hardware and operating system versions
- Hardware warranties for specific hardware

- Specific vendor-supported operating systems and patch levels
- Specific vendor-supported line of business software applications, versions and patch levels
- Specific vendor-supported antivirus, anti-spam and anti-spyware solutions, versions and patch levels
- Specific vendor-supported backup solutions, versions and patch levels
- Remote data storage
- Specific network security protocols and access controls
- Specific broadband requirements
- Other specific 3rd-party vendor relationships

In addition to qualifying the terms under which support will be provided by the outsourced service provider or internal service manager to the end user or client, it is equally important to establish the services that will be considered out of scope and specifically excluded from NOC and Service Desk deliverables and SLAs. Some examples of out of scope services may include:

- Servicing parts, equipment or software not covered by vendor/manufacturer warranty or support
- The cost of any parts, equipment, or shipping charges
- The cost of any software, licensing, or software renewal or upgrade fees

What Should a NOC and Service Desk Support?

- The cost of any 3rd-party vendor or manufacturer support or incident fees required to deliver service
- The cost to bring the end user's or client's environment up to minimum standards required for services
- Failure due to acts of God, building modifications, power failures or other adverse environmental conditions or factors outside of the control of the outsourced service provider or internal service manager
- Service and repair made necessary by the alteration or modification of equipment, operating systems, software applications or services other than that authorized by the outsourced service provider's or internal service manager's NOC or Service Desk staff; including alterations, software installations or modifications of any kind made by end users, the client or their vendors, or anyone other than the outsourced service provider's or internal service manager's NOC or Service Desk staff
- Maintenance of software applications unless specifically included in service agreement and SLA
- Programming (modification of software code) and program (software) unless specifically included in service agreement and SLA
- Training services of any kind

It is important that any and all qualifiers for service such as these be clearly understood by the end user or client prior to engagement and on-boarding by the outsourced service provider or internal service manager. This will reduce misunderstandings and instead improve client satisfaction during service delivery.

Service Agreements and SLAs

Service Agreement Considerations
The outsourced service provider's or internal service
manager's Service Level Agreement (SLA) is the agreement
that binds their level of service between their NOC and Service
Desk deliverables and their end users or clients, and records
the common understanding regarding:

- Services
- Priorities
- Responsibilities
- Guarantees
- Availability
- Serviceability
- Performance
- Operation
- Response
- Resolution

Agreements are commonly written to include SLAs in
specific sections, along with service definitions, and may
include:

- Definition of services
- Term of agreement
- Fees and payment schedule
- Taxes
- Coverage hours

- Exclusions
- Performance measurement
- Incident management process and response time
- Limitation of liability
- Service requirements
- Covered equipment and/or services

The following is an example of an outsourced service provider's Managed Services Agreement and SLA.

Managed Services Agreement and SLA Example

This sample Managed Services Agreement and SLA is included for instructional and informational purposes only, and is not recommended, nor warranted for use.

Always have legal counsel review any and all agreements or documents that you utilize in your IT practice or business unit, or distribute to your end users or clients prior to doing so.

Local laws and liabilities can never be fully covered by any type of generic document, including this sample Managed Services Agreement and SLA.

Managed Services Agreement and SLA

1.   Term of Agreement

This Agreement between

_____, herein referred to as Client, and _____,

hereinafter referred to as Service Provider, is effective upon the date signed, shall remain in force for a period of three years, and be reviewed annually to address any necessary adjustments or modifications. Should adjustments or modifications be required that increase the monthly fees paid for the services rendered under this Agreement, these increases will not exceed _____% of the value of the existing monthly fees due under this Agreement. The Service Agreement automatically renews for a subsequent three year term beginning on the day immediately following the end of the Initial Term, unless either party gives the other ninety (90) days prior written notice of its intent not to renew this Agreement.

a) This Agreement may be terminated by the Client upon ninety (90) days' written notice if the Service Provider:

I.   Fails to fulfill in any material respect its

---

obligations under this Agreement and does not cure such failure within thirty (30) days' of receipt of such written notice.

II. Breaches any material term or condition of this Agreement and fails to remedy such breach within thirty (30) days' of receipt of such written notice.

III. Terminates or suspends its business operations, unless it is succeeded by a permitted assignee under this Agreement.

b) This Agreement may be terminated by the Service Provider upon ninety (90) days written notice to the Client.

c) If either party terminates this Agreement, Service Provider will assist Client in the orderly termination of services, including timely transfer of the services to another designated provider. Client agrees to pay Service Provider the actual costs of rendering such assistance.

---

2. **Fees and Payment Schedule**

   Fees will be $_____ per month, invoiced to Client on a monthly basis, and will become due and payable on the first day of each month. Services will be suspended if payment is not received within 5 days following date due. Refer to Appendix B for services covered by the monthly fee under the terms of this Agreement.

   It is understood that any and all services requested by Client that fall outside of the terms of this Agreement will be considered Projects, and will be quoted and billed as separate, individual Services.

3. **Taxes**

   It is understood that any Federal, State or Local Taxes applicable shall be added to each invoice for services or materials rendered under this Agreement. Client shall pay any such taxes unless a valid exemption certificate is furnished to Service Provider for the state of use.

4. **Coverage**

   Remote Helpdesk and Vendor Management of Client's IT networks will be provided to the Client by Service Provider through remote means between the hours of 8:00 am – 5:00 pm Monday through Friday, excluding public holidays. Network Monitoring Services will be provided 24/7/365. All services qualifying under these conditions, as well as Services that fall outside this scope will fall under the provisions of Appendix B. Hardware costs of any kind are not covered under the terms of this Agreement.

Support and Escalation

Service Provider will respond to Client's Trouble Tickets under the provisions of Appendix A, and with best effort after hours or on holidays. Trouble Tickets must be opened by Client's designated I.T. Contact Person, by email to our Help Desk, or by phone if email is unavailable. Each call will be assigned a Trouble Ticket number for tracking. Our escalation process is detailed in Appendix A.

Service outside Normal Working Hours

Emergency services performed outside of the hours of 8:00 am – 5:00 pm Monday through Friday, excluding public holidays, shall be subject to provisions of Appendix B.

Service Calls Where No Trouble is found

If Client requests onsite service and no problem is found or reproduced, Client shall be billed at the current applicable rates as indicated in Appendix B.

Limitation of Liability

In no event shall Service Provider be held liable for indirect, special, incidental or consequential damages arising out of service provided hereunder, including but not limited to loss of profits or revenue, loss of use of equipment, lost data, costs of substitute equipment, or other costs.

5.   **Additional Maintenance Services**

Hardware/System Support

Service Provider shall provide support of all hardware and systems specified in Appendix B, provided that all Hardware is covered under a currently active vendor support contract; or replaceable parts be readily available, and all Software be Genuine, Currently Licensed and Vendor-Supported. Should any hardware or systems fail to meet these provisions, they will be excluded from this Service Agreement. Should 3rd Party vendor support charges be required in order to resolve

---

any issues, these will be passed on to the Client after first receiving the Client's authorization to incur them.

Virus Recovery for current, licensed Antivirus protected systems

Damages caused by, and recovery from, virus infection not detected and quarantined by the latest Antivirus definitions are covered under the terms of this Agreement. This Service is limited to those systems protected with a currently licensed, vendor-supported Antivirus solution.

Monitoring Services

Service Provider will provide ongoing monitoring and security services of all critical devices as indicated in Appendix B. Service Provider will provide monthly reports as well as document critical alerts, scans and event resolutions to Client. Should a problem be discovered during monitoring, Service Provider shall make every attempt to rectify the condition in a timely manner through remote means.

---

6.   **Suitability of Existing Environment**
Minimum Standards Required for Services

In order for Client's existing environment to qualify for
Service Provider's Managed Services, the following
requirements must be met:

1. All Servers with Microsoft Windows Operating
   Systems must be running Windows 2008 Server
   or later, and have all of the latest Microsoft
   Service Packs and Critical Updates installed.
2. All Desktop PC's and notebooks/laptops with
   Microsoft Windows operating systems must be
   running Windows 7 or later, and have all of the
   latest Microsoft service packs and critical
   updates installed.
3. All Server and Desktop Software must be
   genuine, licensed and vendor-supported.
4. The environment must have a currently
   licensed, up-to-date and vendor-supported
   server-based antivirus solution protecting all
   servers, desktops, notebooks/laptops, and
   email.
5. The environment must have a currently licensed,
   vendor-supported server-based backup solution.

---

6. The environment must have a currently licensed, vendor-supported hardware firewall between the internal network and the Internet.
7. Any Wireless data traffic in the environment must be secured with a minimum of 128bit data encryption.

Costs required to bring Client's environment up to these Minimum Standards are not included in this Agreement.

7. Excluded Services

Service rendered under this Agreement does not include:

1) Parts, equipment or software not covered by vendor/manufacturer warranty or support.
2) The cost of any parts, equipment, or shipping charges of any kind.
3) The cost of any software, licensing, or software renewal or upgrade fees of any kind.
4) The cost of any 3rd party vendor or manufacturer support or incident fees of any kind.

5) The cost to bring Client's environment up to minimum standards required for Services.

6) Failure due to acts of God, building modifications, power failures or other adverse environmental conditions or factors.

7) Service and repair made necessary by the alteration or modification of equipment other than that authorized by Service Provider, including alterations, software installations or modifications of equipment made by Client's employees or anyone other than Service Provider.

8) Maintenance of Applications software packages, whether acquired from Service Provider or any other source unless as specified in Appendix B.

9) Programming (modification of software code) and program (software) maintenance unless as specified in Appendix B.

10) Training Services of any kind.

8. Miscellaneous

This Agreement shall be governed by the laws of the State of _____. It constitutes the entire Agreement between Client and Service Provider for monitoring/maintenance/service of all equipment listed in "Appendix B." Its terms and conditions shall prevail should there be any variance with the terms and conditions of any order submitted by Client.

Service Provider is not responsible for failure to render services due to circumstances beyond its control including, but not limited to, acts of God.

9.   **Acceptance of Service Agreement**

This Service Agreement covers only those services and equipment listed in "Appendix B." Service Provider must deem any equipment/services Client may want to add to this Agreement after the effective date acceptable. The addition of equipment/services not listed in "Appendix B" at the signing of this Agreement, if acceptable to Service Provider, shall result in an adjustment to the Client's monthly charges.

IN WITNESS WHEREOF, the parties hereto have caused this Service Agreement to be signed by their duly authorized representatives as of the date set forth below.

_____

Authorized Signature   Service Provider   Date

_____

Authorized Signature   Client   Date

Managed Services Agreement

Appendix A

Response and Resolution Times

The following table shows the targets of response and resolution times for each priority level:

Trouble	Priority	Response time (in hours) *	Resolution time (in hours) *	Escalation threshold (in hours)
Service not available (all users and functions unavailable).	1	Within 1 hour	ASAP – Best Effort	2 hours
Significant degradation of service (large number of users or business critical functions affected)	2	Within 4 hours	ASAP – Best Effort	4 hours
Limited degradation of service (limited number of users or functions affected, business process can continue).	3	Within 24 hours	ASAP – Best Effort	48 hours
Small service degradation (business process can continue, one user affected).	4	within 48 hours	ASAP – Best Effort	96 hours

---

Support Tiers

The following details and describes our Support Tier levels:

Support Tier	Description
Tier 1 Support	All support incidents begin in Tier 1, where the initial trouble ticket is created, the issue is identified and clearly documented, and basic hardware/software troubleshooting is initiated.
Tier 2 Support	All support incidents that cannot be resolved with Tier 1 Support are escalated to Tier 2, where more complex support on hardware/software issues can be provided by more experienced Engineers.
Tier 3 Support	Support Incidents that cannot be resolved by Tier 2 Support are escalated to Tier 3, where support is provided by the most qualified and experienced Engineers who have the ability to collaborate with 3rd Party (Vendor) Support Engineers to resolve the most complex issues.

Managed Services Agreement

Appendix A (cont)

Service Request Escalation Procedure

1. Support Request is Received

2. Trouble Ticket is Created

3. Issue is Identified and documented in Help Desk system

4. Issue is qualified to determine if it can be resolved through Tier 1 Support

   If issue can be resolved through Tier 1 Support:

5. Level 1 Resolution - issue is worked to successful resolution

6. Quality Control –Issue is verified to be resolved to Client's satisfaction

7. Trouble Ticket is closed, after complete problem resolution details have been updated in Help Desk system

   If issue cannot be resolved through Tier 1 Support:

6. Issue is escalated to Tier 2 Support

---

7. Issue is qualified to determine if it can be resolved by Tier 2 Support

   If issue can be resolved through Tier 2 Support:

8. Level 2 Resolution - issue is worked to successful resolution

9. Quality Control –Issue is verified to be resolved to Client's satisfaction

10. Trouble Ticket is closed, after complete problem resolution details have been updated in Help Desk system

    If issue cannot be resolved through Tier 2 Support:

9. Issue is escalated to Tier 3 Support

10. Issue is qualified to determine if it can be resolved through Tier 3 Support

    If issue can be resolved through Tier 3 Support:

11. Level 3 Resolution - issue is worked to successful resolution

12. Quality Control –Issue is verified to be resolved to Client's satisfaction

---

13. Trouble Ticket is closed, after complete problem resolution details have been updated in Help Desk system

If issue cannot be resolved through Tier 3 Support:

12. Issue is escalated to Onsite Support
13. Issue is qualified to determine if it can be resolved through Onsite Support

If issue can be resolved through Onsite Support:

14. Onsite Resolution - issue is worked to successful resolution
15. Quality Control –Issue is verified to be resolved to Client's satisfaction
16. Trouble Ticket is closed, after complete problem resolution details have been updated in Help Desk system

If issue cannot be resolved through Onsite Support:

17. I.T. Manager Decision Point – request is updated with complete details of all activity performed

Managed Services Agreement

Appendix B

Description	Frequency	Included in Maintenance
General		
Document software and hardware changes	As performed	YES
Test backups with restores	Monthly	YES
Monthly reports of work accomplished, work in progress, etc.	Monthly	YES
Systems		
Check print queues	As needed	YES
Ensure that all server services are running	Daily/hourly	YES
Keep Service Packs, Patches and Hotfixes current as per company policy	Monthly	YES
Check event log of every server and identify any potential issues	As things appear	YES
Monitor hard drive free space on server, clients	Daily/hourly	YES
Reboot servers if needed	As needed	YES
Run defrag and chkdsk on all drives	As needed	YES
Scheduled off time server maintenance	As needed	YES
Install software upgrades	As needed	YES
Determine logical directory structure, Implement, MAP, and detail	Revisit Monthly	YES
Set up and maintain groups (accounting, admin, printers, sales, warehouse, etc)	As needed	YES
Check status of backup and restores	Daily	YES
Alert office manager to dangerous conditions -Memory running low -Hard drive showing sign of failure -Hard drive running out of disk space -Controllers losing interrupts -Network Cards report unusual collision activity	As needed	YES
Educate and correct user errors (deleted files, corrupted files, etc.)	As needed	YES
Clean and prune directory structure, keep efficient and active	Monthly	YES
Disaster Recovery		
Disaster Recovery of Server(s)	As Needed	YES

Managed Services Agreement
Appendix B (cont.)

Networks

Check router logs	Weekly	YES
Performance Monitoring/Capacity Planning	Weekly	YES
Monitor DSU/TSU, switches, hubs and internet connectivity, and make sure everything is operational (available for SNMP manageable devices only)	Weekly	YES
Major SW/HW upgrades to network backbone, including routers, WAN additions, etc.	As needed	YES
Maintain office connectivity to the Internet	Ongoing	YES

Security

Check firewall logs	Monthly	YES
Confirm that antivirus virus definition auto updates have occurred	As Needed	YES
Confirm that virus updates have occurred	As Needed	YES
Confirm that backup has been performed on a daily basis	Daily	YES
Create new directories, shares and security groups, new accounts, disable/delete old accounts, manage account policies	As Needed	YES
Permissions and file system management	As Needed	YES
Set up new users including login restrictions, passwords, security, applications	As needed	YES
Set up and change security for users and applications	As needed	YES
Monitor for unusual activity among users	Ongoing	YES

Apps

Exchange user/mailbox management	As needed	YES
Monitor directory replication	As needed	YES
Monitor WINS replication	As needed	YES
SQL server management	As needed	YES
Overall application disk space management	As needed	YES
Ensure Microsoft Office Applications are functioning as designed	As needed	YES

Appendix "B" Cont.

Service Rates	
Labor	Rate
Remote PC Management/Help Desk - 8am-5pm M-F	INCLUDED
Remote Printer Management - 8am-5pm M-F	INCLUDED
Remote Network Management - 8am-5pm M-F	INCLUDED
Remote Server Management - 8am-5pm M-F	INCLUDED
24x7x365 Network Monitoring	INCLUDED
Lab Labor - 8am-5pm M-F	INCLUDED
Onsite Labor - 8am-5pm M-F	INCLUDED
Remote PC Management/Help Desk - 5:01pm-9pm M-F	$_____/hr
Remote Printer Management - 5:01pm-9pm M-F	$_____/hr
Remote Network Management - 5:01pm-9pm M-F	$_____/hr
Remote Server Management - 5:01pm-9pm M-F	$_____/hr
Lab Labor - 5:01pm-9pm M-F	$_____/hr
Onsite Labor - 5:01pm-9pm M-F	$_____/hr
Remote Labor All Other Times	$_____/hr
Lab Labor All Other Times	$_____/hr
Onsite Labor All Other Times	$_____/hr

Covered Equipment		
Managed Desktops:		(Desktops & Notebooks)
Managed Printers:		
Managed Networks:		
Managed Servers:		
Managed Cell/PDA:		(Smart phones & PDAs)

Section 4: Processes

In order for the outsourced service provider's or internal service manager's NOC and Service Desks to deliver uniform, measurable services in adherence to established SLAs; and provide end users or clients with a consistent, satisfactory support experience, they need to develop, implement and hold their staff accountable to effective service delivery processes and procedures.

In this context, these NOC and Service Desk service delivery processes are defined as those processes and workflows which are necessary in order to allow the NOC and Service Desk the ability to effectively deliver scheduled and unscheduled services to end users or clients efficiently, and include:

- Responding to alert conditions and service requests
- Following best practices for incident management and resolution
- Delivering services within established SLA's

These service delivery processes govern the following scheduled and unscheduled events:

- Remote support
- Onsite support

In addition, these service delivery processes include a documented procedure for addressing any and all activity performed by the NOC and Service Desk during service delivery, and embodies a workflow which easily directs the NOC or Service Desk resource throughout the service delivery process.

Specific processes that the outsourced service provider or internal service manager will develop and implement for effective NOC and Service Desk service delivery may include:

- End User or Client On-Boarding, Provisioning and Service Turn-Up/Go-Live
- Incident Management
- Problem Management
- Configuration Management
- Change Management
- Release Management
- Risk Management
- Service Level Management
- Service Financial Management
- Capacity Management
- Service Continuity Management

- Availability Management
- Security Management
- Communication Management
- Reporting Management
- Customer Satisfaction Management

We will cover end user or client on-boarding, provisioning and turn-up/go-live in Section 5 – Clients, and discuss the rest of these processes in the following chapters.

Incident and Problem Management

The Difference Between Incident Management and Problem Management

Although both incidents and problems are related, and will each trigger an automated alert or an end user or client-generated service request, they are different, and are responded to and handled differently by the outsourced service provider's or internal service manager's NOC and Service Desk.

In this context, an incident can be anything that degrades or interrupts the end user's or client's information technology-supported business processes, activities and workflows.

The purpose of Incident Management is to restore business continuity as quickly as possible.

A problem, in contrast, is simply a recurring incident.

The purpose of Problem Management is to determine the root cause of recurring incidents.

With this understanding, it makes sense that the manner in which the NOC or Service Desk responds to, and the processes they employ to resolve these issues may differ.

ITIL (Information Technology Infrastructure Library), a comprehensive set of concepts and best practices for IT Service Management, separates the incident management process into six unique components:

1. Incident detection and recording
2. Classification and initial support
3. Analysis and diagnosis
4. Resolution and recovery
5. Incident closure
6. Incident ownership, monitoring, tracking and communication

After a service request has been created, documented, prioritized and assigned to a queue or resource in the Professional Services Automation solution; either as the result of an alert triggered by the Remote Monitoring and Management tool or directly generated by an end user or client, an outsourced service provider's or internal service manager's Incident Management Process will be followed to address the service request.

Adhering to the outsourced service provider's or internal service manager's Change Management, Configuration Management and Communication Management processes, the NOC or Service Desk resource assigned to the service request will employ the outsourced service provider's or internal service manager's Incident Management Process, which may resemble the following:

1. Support request is received

2. Service request is created

3. Issue is Identified, documented, prioritized and assigned in Professional Services Automation solution

4. Issue is qualified to determine if it can be resolved through Tier 1 Support

   If issue can be resolved through Tier 1 Support:

5. Level 1 Resolution - issue is worked to successful resolution

6. Quality Control - Issue is verified to be resolved to end user's or client's satisfaction

7. Service request is closed, after complete resolution details have been updated in Professional Services Automation solution

   If issue cannot be resolved through Tier 1 Support:

6. Issue is escalated to Tier 2 Support

---

7. Issue is qualified to determine if it can be resolved by Tier 2 Support

    If issue can be resolved through Tier 2 Support:

8. Level 2 Resolution - issue is worked to successful resolution

9. Quality Control - Issue is verified to be resolved to end user's or client's satisfaction

10. Service request is closed, after complete resolution details have been updated in Professional Services Automation solution

    If issue cannot be resolved through Tier 2 Support:

9. Issue is escalated to Tier 3 Support

10. Issue is qualified to determine if it can be resolved through Tier 3 Support

    If issue can be resolved through Tier 3 Support:

11. Level 3 Resolution - issue is worked to successful resolution

12. Quality Control - Issue is verified to be resolved to end user's or client's satisfaction

---

---

13. Service request is closed, after complete resolution details have been updated in Professional Services Automation solution

    If issue cannot be resolved through Tier 3 Support:

11. Issue is escalated to onsite support

12. Issue is qualified to determine if it can be resolved through onsite support

    If issue can be resolved through Onsite Support:

14. Onsite resolution - issue is worked to successful resolution

15. Quality Control - Issue is verified to be resolved to end user's or client's satisfaction

16. Service request is closed, after complete resolution details have been updated in Professional Services Automation solution

    If issue cannot be resolved through Onsite Support:

17. I.T. Manager Decision Point – request is updated with complete details of all activity performed

---

1. • Receipt - Service request is received

2. • Creation - Trouble ticket is created

3. • Identification - Issue is identified, documented, prioritized and assigned

4. • Qualification - Issue is qualified to determine if it can be resolved in Tier 1

If issue can be resolved in Tier 1:

5. • IMR- Issue is worked to successful resolution

6. • QC – Issue is verified to be resolved to client satisfaction

7. • Close – Issue is closed after complete IMR activities are documented in PSA

If issue cannot be resolved in Tier 1:

6
- Escalation - Issue is escalated to Tier 2

7
- Qualification - Issue is qualified to determine if it can be resolved in Tier 2

If issue can be resolved through Tier 2 Support:

8
- IMR- Issue is worked to successful resolution

9
- QC – Issue is verified to be resolved to client satisfaction

10
- Close – Issue is closed after complete IMR activities are documented in PSA

If issue cannot be resolved through Tier 2 Support:

9
- Escalation - Issue is escalated to Tier 3

10
- Qualification - Issue is qualified to determine if it can be resolved in Tier 3

If issue can be resolved through Tier 3 Support:

11
- IMR- Issue is worked to successful resolution

12
- QC – Issue is verified to be resolved to client satisfaction

13
- Close – Issue is closed after complete IMR activities are documented in PSA

If issue cannot be resolved through Tier 3 Support:

12 • Escalation - Issue is escalated to onsite support

13 • Qualification - Issue is qualified to determine if it can be resolved through onsite support

If issue can be resolved through Onsite Support:

14 • IMR- Issue is worked to successful resolution

15 • QC – Issue is verified to be resolved to client satisfaction

16 • Close – Issue is closed after complete IMR activities are documented in PSA

If issue cannot be resolved through Onsite Support:

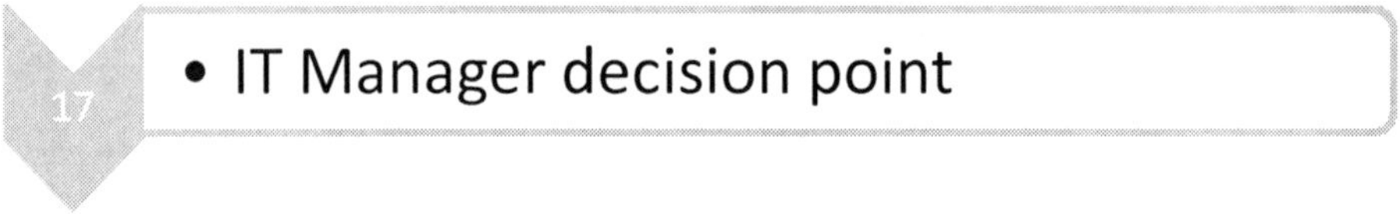

• IT Manager decision point

17

Figure 23 – Incident Management Process

As discussed, should an incident recur, it becomes classified as a problem, and the outsourced service provider's or internal service manager's Problem Management process must be initiated.

The function of problem management is to:

1. Investigate the root cause of recurring incidents
2. Classify the problem as a known error
3. Determine possible solutions
4. Analyze the impact of the solution
5. Implement the remediation solution
6. Review post-remediation impact

A problem is classified as a known error when its underlying cause has been identified. This is the result of the analysis conducted and is the outcome necessary in order to determine possible solutions for remediation.

Adhering to the outsourced service provider's or internal service manager's Change Management, Configuration Management and Communication Management processes, the NOC or Service Desk resource assigned to the service

---

request for the problem will employ the outsourced service provider's or internal service manager's Problem Management Process, which may resemble the following:

1. Support request is received
2. Service request is created, or closed service request for initial incident is re-opened
3. Issue is identified and documented in Professional Services Automation solution as a Problem
4. Issue is analyzed to determine root cause of problem
5. Issue is classified as a known error
6. The impact of possible solutions are evaluated and the best solution is determined
7. A request for change is initiated per outsourced service provider's or internal service manager's Change Management process
8. Change is implemented
9. Quality Control - Issue is monitored and verified to be resolved to end user's or client's satisfaction

---

10. Service request is closed, after complete resolution details have been updated in Professional Services Automation solution

1. • Receipt - Service request is received

2. • Creation - Trouble ticket is created

3. • Identification - Issue is identified and documented

4. • Qualification - Issue is qualified to determine if it can be resolved in Tier 1

5. • Issue is classified as known error

6. • Impact evaluated and solution determined

7. • Request for Change

8. • Change implemented

9. • QC - Issue is verified to be resolved to client satisfaction

10. • Close – Issue is closed after complete PMR activities are documented in PSA

Figure 24 – Problem Management Process

Configuration, Change and Release Management

The Differences Between Configuration, Change and Release Management

Configuration, Change and Release Management are three individual processes that are also closely related and used in concert with each other in many instances during NOC and Service Desk service delivery.

Plainly stated, Configuration Management embodies those processes that govern the collection, documentation, maintenance and updating of configuration data in end user or client IT infrastructures, and the management of that information in a Configuration Management Database. Many Professional Services Automation solutions support this management capability.

The purpose of Configuration Management is to insure that all configuration data governing hardware, operating system, application software and services components of an IT Infrastructure are documented, maintained and updated as changes are made over time.

Configuration Management of a typical end user's or client's IT infrastructure may include managing the documented configurations of:

- Hardware, including servers, desktops, laptops, routers, switches, firewalls, Smartphones, PDAs and other devices
- Operating systems
- Application software
- Services including broadband, voice, VoIP, etc.
- Live and printed documentation

Change Management represents those standardized processes that govern all changes made by the NOC or Service Desk to end user or client hardware, operating systems, software applications and services during service delivery. These activities are also documented in the outsourced service provider's or internal service manager's Professional Services Automation solution, which may help automate the creation and approval of change requests during proactive maintenance and reactive incident and problem management activity.

The purpose of Change Management is to insure that change is planned properly and standardized processes and procedures are utilized to initiate change in an efficient manner that reduces the impact of change to the end user or client.

Akin to Configuration Management, Change Management of a typical end user's or client's IT infrastructure may include managing changes made to:

- Hardware, including servers, desktops, laptops, routers, switches, firewalls, smartphones, PDAs and other devices
- Operating systems and patches, updates, service packs, hotfixes, etc.
- Application software and patches, updates, service packs, hotfixes, etc.
- Services including broadband, voice, VoIP, connectivity, etc.
- Network and other documentation
- Disaster recovery and business continuity plans

Release Management relies heavily on Configuration and Change Management, and is responsible for the implementation and quality control of all hardware, operating system, software application and services; and version updates, upgrades and new releases before they are introduced into the end user's or client's production environment.

The purpose of Release Management is to insure that the introduction of new major or minor hardware or software releases into a production environment is planned properly

---

and evaluated in a test environment prior to its rollout to minimize the impact of the introduction to the end user or client.

Release Management in a typical end user's or client's IT infrastructure may include application to:

- Hardware, including servers, desktops, laptops, routers, switches, firewalls, smartphones, PDAs and other devices
- Operating systems and patches, updates, service packs, hotfixes, etc.
- Application software and patches, updates, service packs, hotfixes, etc.
- Services including broadband, voice, VoIP, connectivity, etc.

Risk Management

Risk Versus Reward

In this context, Risk Management processes utilized by the outsourced service provider's or internal service manager's NOC and Service Desk embody the identification and assessment of potential risks during service delivery, and the strategies utilized to minimize, monitor for and control the probability or impact of negative outcomes to the end user or client.

Strategies for managing risk may include:

- Identifying the potential for risk
- Characterizing potential risks
- Assessing potential risks to specific activities
- Determining the result of risk
- Discovering or identifying ways to reduce risk
- Creating a strategy to reduce risk based on prioritized risk reduction procedures

Risk Management is a necessary process during normal day to day NOC and Service Desk service delivery, and must be conducted throughout proactive maintenance, as well as reactive Incident, Problem and Change and Release Management activities. The mitigation of risk is a key component in minimizing impact to the end user or client during these activities.

Let's explore an example situation and apply Risk Management to a common end user or client scenario. Let's say that a service request has been generated by an end user reporting that they cannot access the Internet. The outsourced service provider's or internal service manager's Service Desk resource reviews the information in the service request and works directly with the end user through the Remote Monitoring and Management tool's Remote Access and Control capabilities to share and control their desktop to conduct the following activities:

1. Verify network card configuration
2. Verify ability to release/renew IP address within correct DHCP scope and correct DNS entries

This all looks good, so the next activity conducted may be:

3. Ping the internal gateway – response is good
4. Ping an external IP address – response is good

This verifies the ability to reach internal and external devices by IP address, so the next activity might be:

5. Ping external URL – response times out
6. Ping internal device by host name – response is good

Now we're getting somewhere. But up to this point evaluation of risk has not identified the necessity to modify the troubleshooting process, as it has simply been benign activity

---

conducted during Incident Management to identify the cause of the incident, and no change has been implemented other than releasing and renewing the device's IP address – an activity that occurs normally. Next steps may include:

7. Verify ability to ping external IP addresses and inability to ping any external URLs

The suspicion now becomes an issue with DNS. The next activity to isolate DNS as the area to focus on may include:

8. Configure the device's network adapter with an internal static IP and external DNS address
9. Ping an external IP address – response is good
10. Ping an external URL – response is good

So there appears to be a potential issue with the DNS server addresses being leased to this particular device. But why just this device? There have been no other reports of this particular issue from any of the other users in the environment. More information reveals that this is the only user in the office using a laptop today with a wireless connection. So next steps may include:

11. Remotely access the device managing DHCP services for wired and wireless devices on the user's network

---

---

12. Review the DHCP configuration for the wireless network and compare the DNS server settings against those being leased to the wired network

It is discovered that the DNS server settings between the wired and wireless networks do not match.

Since this is the first report of this issue, establishing this service request as an incident, the Service Desk's responsibility is to restore business continuity for this user as quickly as possible. The first proposed change to reach this goal would be to change the DNS server setting for the wireless network to match those used for the wired network on the device handing out leases, wouldn't it?

...and here is where Configuration Management, Change Management and Risk Management meet during the Incident Management process:

- The Service Desk employs Incident Management during the process of restoring business continuity for the end user
- The Service Desk employs Configuration Management to determine the configuration of all devices involved in the Incident Management process
- The Service Desk will modify device configurations during the Incident Management process

---

- The Service Desk must evaluate risk prior to requesting or implementing change through the Risk Management process

So what is the risk that needs to be evaluated in this scenario? Well, in order to modify the DNS server settings on the device managing DHCP services for the wired and wireless networks in the user's environment – the gateway router – a reboot of the device will be required...

Remember our basic Risk Management strategy? Here it is applied to this specific example:

- **Identify the potential for risk** – oh yes, there is absolutely a definite potential for risk
- **Characterize potential risks** - major
- **Assess potential risks to specific activities** – the risk is related to rebooting the gateway router
- **Determine the result of risk** – the result will be to disconnect all users from their existing LAN and WAN sessions
- **Discover or identify ways to reduce risk** – allow the affected user to work with static IP and DNS address settings until a reboot of the gateway router is possible, determine if the user can use a wired connection until the gateway router can be rebooted,

---

determine if the user needs WAN or Internet access until the gateway router can be rebooted

- **Create a strategy to reduce risk based on prioritized risk reduction procedures** – the best solution may be to have the user patch their laptop into the nearest network drop until the gateway router can be rebooted after production hours, as this will not require another support session to reset the wireless network card's static configuration to dynamic after the user is done for the day, a second option would be to use static addressing and initiate the additional support session as described, and the third option might be to have the user work locally until a router reboot is possible

Assuming the first option is implemented, the user is instructed by the Service Desk where to find a network cable and how to patch in to the wired network. The Service Desk manages configuration and change for the gateway router per the outsourced service provider's or internal service manager's policies and procedures, documents all Incident Management activity in the Professional Services Automation solution and schedules the gateway router reboot after hours. During the QA process the next day, the affected user is contacted to verify if their issue has been resolved and receive authorization to close the service request.

Service Level Management

Delivering Services to Support SLAs

In this context, Service Level Management is comprised of those processes, procedures and activities that manage and govern the delivery of NOC and Service Desk services to meet agreed-upon SLAs, or Service Level Agreements; and are focused on the client – as opposed to Service Desk services whose focus is the individual end user.

In order to conduct effective Service Level Management, the outsourced service provider or internal service manager must conduct an effective business needs analysis in order to properly align deliverables with client needs, then continuously monitor and modify those deliverables to insure they meet the established SLA with the client.

The Service Level Management process insures that NOC and Service Desk services are delivered according to SLA

A properly configured Professional Services Automation solution alone is not enough to support effective Service Level Management – the outsourced service provider's or internal service manager's NOC and Service Desk resources must properly deliver services and document all of their activity within it according to the provider's or manager's established service delivery procedures. Only then can meaningful reporting be generated to evaluate performance against SLA.

Service Financial Management

Helping End Users and Clients Afford Technology Services
In this context, Service Level Management is comprised of those processes, procedures and activities that the outsourced service provider or internal service manager employs to identify, reduce and manage the costs associated with their deliverables in order to make them cost-effective for their clients.

The Service Level Management process is employed to evaluate and control IT service delivery costs to insure affordability for clients

Ways to achieve this goal may include:

- Reducing business costs
- Increasing internal efficiencies

In order to reduce business costs, the outsourced service provider or internal service manager may evaluate the following expenses:

- Capital equipment
- Vehicle expenses
- Tools
- IT
- General office and operation expenses

- Labor
- Marketing
- Insurance
- Professional fees
- Sales

In order to increase efficiencies, the outsourced service provider or internal service manager may invest in tools and technologies such as Remote Monitoring and Management, Professional Services Automation and Voice Communications solutions. When integrated and configured properly, this suite of solutions can automate the delivery of many otherwise time and labor-intensive manual processes, create and facilitate an environment of process and workflow standardization and improved communications and deliver meaningful reporting to help evaluate and improve performance and increase service delivery efficiencies.

Over time, a constant review of these cost-reducing and efficiency-improving activities will continue to help the outsourced service provider or internal service manager to manage or drive down costs, allowing these Service Financial Management processes to benefit clients through the ability to receive competitively priced services.

Capacity Management

Right-Sizing Infrastructure and Services for Growth
In this context, Capacity Management is comprised of those processes, procedures and activities that the outsourced service provider or internal service manager employs to insure that their service capacity is scalable to support their own growing client base as well as their end users' or clients' growth.

The Capacity Management process insures that NOC and Service Desk services are scalable to meet internal and external performance needs cost-effectively.

In order to properly optimally align service deliverable capabilities to end user or client business needs economically, the outsourced service provider or internal service manager must:

- Insure the capacity to meet existing end user or client SLAs
- Monitor the performance of deliverables and the infrastructure supporting the NOC and Service Desk
- Monitor the performance of the end user's or client's infrastructure
- Accurately forecast, plan for and implement activities to support increasing capacity needs

---

The outsourced service provider or internal service manager may evaluate and monitor the following internal and end user or client-impacting criteria:

- Application performance
- Workload performance
- Demand performance
- Resource performance
- Hardware performance

In many cases, the outsourced service provider or internal service manager will leverage the capabilities of the Remote Monitoring and Management tool to provide meaningful performance reports to assist in Capacity Management processes and activities.

Service Continuity Management

Recovery from Service Interruption

In this context, Service Continuity Management is comprised of those processes, procedures and activities that the outsourced service provider or internal service manager employs to provide recovery from interruption of IT services and restore business process continuity for the end user or client. Should an interruption in fact occur, Service Continuity processes will be followed by the outsourced service provider's or internal service manager's NOC and Service Desk to restore normal IT and IT-supported business functions.

Service Continuity Management is akin to Disaster Recovery and a precursor to Disaster Recovery or Business Continuity Planning.

The Service Continuity Management process insures that IT and IT-related business operations can recover in the event of interruption or disaster.

In order to insure the high availability of IT and IT-related business processes, and depending upon their SLA, the outsourced service provider or the internal service manager may develop and implement strategies to insure their end user's or client's service continuity in the event of interruption or disaster. This Service Continuity process must incorporate all of the recovery steps necessary to support the restoration of critical IT services and their supported business functions for the end user or client.

Availability Management

When Do You Want It?
In this context, Availability Management is comprised of those processes, procedures and activities that the outsourced service provider or internal service manager employs to insure availability of the end user's or client's IT and IT-supported business functions and services. Availability Management requires continual monitoring, optimizing and management of critical devices, operating systems, application software and services, making a properly configured and operating Remote Monitoring and Management tool a must to deliver services and insure availability cost-effectively.

The Availability Management process insures the reliability, availability, serviceability, resilience and security of the end user's or client's IT and IT-supported services and business functions.

Effective Availability Management is a requirement for the outsourced service provider's or internal service manager's NOC and Service Desk to maintain end user or client SLAs.

Security Management

Is Information Safe?

In this context, Security Management is comprised of those processes, procedures and activities that the outsourced service provider or internal service manager employs to insure the confidentiality, integrity and availability of their own internal, as well as their end user's or client's information, or data. This obviously requires securing much more than simply the information itself, but also the physical hosts of the information, the means of accessing the information, the transport of the information and the personnel authorized to access the information.

The Security Management process insures the confidentiality, integrity and availability of information.

A Security Plan establishes the level of security required to support the outsourced service provider's or internal service manager's internal, as well as end user or client-facing SLAs.

Effective Security Management requires the establishment of a Security Policy which defines:

- The relationship with the outsourced service provider's or their end user's or client's general business policy
- Coordination with other internal and external IT processes

- Rules governing access to information
- Risk assessment procedures
- The security monitoring policy
- The status reporting process
- The scope of the Security Plan
- The structure, processes and procedures of the Security Management process
- The resources responsible for administering the Security Management process
- The internal and external security auditors
- Other supporting resources including hardware, software and staff – including the outsourced service provider's or internal service manager's staff as well as end user's or client's staff

The integrity and security of information is a top priority for many business owners and organizations. Executing an effective Security Management process by the outsourced service provider or internal service manager will deliver value to end users or clients above and beyond NOC and Service Desk deliverables. On the other hand, failing to deliver an effective Security Management process may harm the end user or client so severely that it could jeopardize the continuity or survivability of their business.

Communication Management

Can You Hear Me Now?

In this context, Communication Management is comprised of those processes, procedures and activities that the outsourced service provider or internal service manager employs to foster effective, efficient internal and end user or client-facing communications.

Effective Communication Management is critical in maintaining internal efficiencies and evaluating and improving client satisfaction – especially for the Service Desk.

In addition, since communication in all of its varied forms is such a vital component in the creation and maintenance of a pleasant work environment and culture; which is reflected in the outsourced service provider's or internal service manager's staff's interaction with end users or clients, it is beneficial to help them build awareness, strengthen interpersonal skills and reinforce best practices for communications through an established Communication Management process.

Communication Management governs the content, delivery, timing and means of delivery of all internal and external channels of communication within and without an organization.

Communications governed by an outsourced service provider's or internal service manager's Communications Management process may encompass:

- Verbal communications
  - Face to face
  - Telephonic
  - Voicemail
- Nonverbal communications
  - Facial expressions
  - Body language/bearing
  - Style of dress
- Written communications
  - Email
  - Instant Message
  - Text Message
  - Letters
  - Faxes
  - Reports
  - Minutes
  - Agendas
  - Memos
  - White boards
  - Pin up/cork boards
  - Written Phone messages
  - Pictures/photos/images

- o Website
- o Newsletter

Interpersonal communications may be conducted by the outsourced service provider's or internal service manager's NOC and Service Desk staff with another staff member, a group, or an end user, client or groups of these, and this interpersonal communication can be delivered through written, verbal and nonverbal means. Thus, the staff member must be mindful of the following:

- Who they are communicating with
    - o Role
    - o Status
    - o Culture
- What must be, or is being communicated
    - o Confidential/proprietary information
    - o Bad news
    - o Good news
    - o Gossip
    - o Instructions
    - o Other
- The delivery mechanism for the communication
    - o Verbal
    - o Written
- The manner in which the communication will be delivered

Communication Management

- o Face to face
- o Telephonically
- o Voicemail
- o Email, IM, text, letter, fax, report

Based upon any combination of these comprising an everyday communications scenario, you can quickly appreciate the value of establishing rules for the transfer or dissemination of information down to a granular level that may include the formatting and verbiage used in written correspondence – and even what is appropriate to write on a white board, pin up on a cork board or send as a photo or email attachment electronically.

This type of cultural awareness embodied in the outsourced service provider's or internal service manager's communication protocols will establish the ground rules for their staff's communications behavior and suit them well during their service delivery activities with end users or clients.

In order to insure adherence to these protocols, the outsourced service provider or internal service manager must monitor their staff's adherence to the communications standards they have established through the Communication Management process, and hold them accountable to them.

Section 5: Clients

In order for the outsourced service provider's or internal service manager's NOC and Service Desks to deliver uniform, measurable services in adherence to established SLAs; and provide end users or clients with a consistent, satisfactory support experience, they need to develop, implement and hold their staff accountable to effective qualification, on-boarding and ongoing service delivery and customer satisfaction processes and procedures.

Client Qualifications for Service

Setting Minimum Client Qualifications for Service

Not all clients will qualify for the outsourced service provider's or internal service manager's NOC and Service Desk services – *nor should they.*

In order for the outsourced service provider or internal service manager to deliver services effectively, efficiently and profitably, not only do minimum standards need to be established for the IT infrastructure to be managed, *but for potential clients as well.*

Holding true to these client standards can mean the difference between building strong, growing, mutually beneficial business relationships with clients – or being contractually obligated to deliver services to difficult, noisy, slow-paying *customers* that do not value the time, dedication and effort required to support their infrastructure and users.

Choosing to support the wrong client will cost the outsourced service provider or internal service manager more time and money than it is worth – and burden them and their NOC and Service Desk staff with unnecessary bottlenecks and frustration.

Best in class providers may consider the following when determining a potential client's suitability for services:

- Prior history and experience with other providers and vendors
- Financial suitability, standing and creditworthiness
- Years in business
- Staff attrition
- Client's perception and value of the service relationship
- Existence of, or willingness to create an IT budget
- Availability of; and direct access to, decision makers
- Willingness to provide necessary discovery information and access to key staff prior to formalizing a service agreement
- Willingness to invest to bring existing IT infrastructure up to minimum standards required for service

The client's history with other vendors; and specifically IT providers, will be a good initial indicator of their perception of the value of support services. If they feel that the price to be paid to maintain their infrastructure and support their users is an annoyance and necessary evil to maintain their business, and they have an unusually active history of hiring and firing IT service providers, as well as a high staff turnover rate – these are obvious red flags to consider.

On the other hand, if the client perceives the cost of supporting their environment and users as an investment that provides them a competitive advantage in their industry or target market, and have an existing IT budget; or are willing to create one, these are good signs.

Unfortunately, in many cases the internal service manager will not have much influence in qualifying their own clients or end users prior to delivering service, as their role may be to support their own organization's internal infrastructure and users. If this is the case; when faced with difficult end users or internal decision makers, the service manager must find ways to reverse any negative end user or client perceptions regarding their IT support services.

This can also serve the outsourced service provider when dealing with difficult existing client or end user situations, but the best way to address this potential reality is to qualify prospects carefully to avoid engaging with difficult clients in the first place when possible.

Methods of reversing negative end user or client perceptions may include:

- Reviewing and revising end user or client-facing service delivery processes and procedures to improve interpersonal effectiveness
- Communicating more, and more effectively with end users and clients

- Increasing anonymous customer satisfaction surveys and polling to identify areas for improvement – and improving them
- Sharing good news with clients and end users, such as adherence to SLAs, positive testimonials or comments and improved customer service metrics
- Increasing face-to-face strategic meetings with the decision maker and discussing historical performance, positive improvements and future goals and plans to achieve them
- Understanding the decision maker's monthly, quarterly, and year-over-year goals and reflecting service alignment, support and value in helping to realize those goals

In today's society; where electronic communications fostered by email, Facebooking, blogging, tweeting and texting makes it easy to reduce verbal communications between individuals, the astute outsourced service provider or internal service manager will redouble their staff's efforts at increasing their verbal communications with end users and clients.

Relationships are built and improved upon through verbal interpersonal interaction, not electronic communications, and since by their very nature, NOC and Service Desk services are delivered remotely; and end users, clients and the outsourced service provider's or internal service manager's staff may

---

never have the opportunity to physically meet each other, it is vitally important to seek out ways to provide as much of a human touch as possible, whenever possible.

Infrastructure Qualifications for Service

Setting Minimum Infrastructure Qualifications for Service
In order to maximize service delivery efficiencies, effectiveness, customer satisfaction and profitability, standardizing on and enforcing baseline environmental qualifications for the type and state of hardware, operating systems, applications software and services supported will serve the outsourced service provider or internal service manager well. Although it may be more challenging for the internal service manager to enforce some of these requirements initially, over time it may be possible for them to establish and achieve a baseline standard within their internal organization.

Standardizing on minimum environmental qualifications in order to qualify for service allows the outsourced service provider or internal service manager to maintain their staff's training requirements, certification levels and support specializations on a specific number of products and services. Instead of trying to support everything under the sun; which is impossible to do, and a great way to miss SLAs and erode client confidence and satisfaction as a result, the enforcement of minimum standards for service; along with the establishment of supported products and services, improves service delivery effectiveness and customer satisfaction.

Hardware and Hardware Devices

In order to achieve standardization across hardware devices, the outsourced service provider or internal service manager may consider the following and establish specific baseline requirements based upon the role of the hardware or device in the infrastructure:

- Type of hardware (server, router, firewall, switch, pc, laptop, Smartphone, etc.)
- Brand of hardware
- A specific CPU type and speed
- A minimum amount of physical RAM
- A specific amount of free HDD space
- A specific BIOS type and level
- Specific physical connectivity types
- Specific local and remote connectivity methods
- Supported protocols and ports
- Physical security
- Access rights and security
- Specific configuration
- Specific WAN/LAN/DMZ Location
- Interoperability with other local or remote devices
- Hardware redundancy
- Warranty

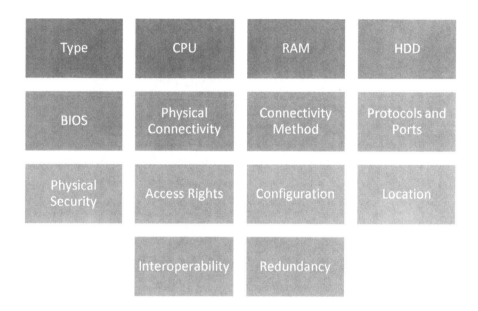

Figure25 – Minimum Hardware Requirements for Service

Operating Systems and Applications Software

In order to achieve standardization across operating system and application software, the outsourced service provider or internal service manager may consider the following and establish specific baseline requirements based upon the role of the operating system or application software in the infrastructure:

- A specific operating system type, version and patch level (server, desktop, Smartphone, etc.)

- A specific Software application type, version and patch level (operating system, line of business, office productivity, etc.)
- Specific configuration
- Local and remote connectivity methods
- Supported protocols and ports
- Security methods
- Interoperability and ability to communicate with other local or remote systems, services, functions, databases and applications
- Service availability and redundancy
- Data backup, restore and business continuity processes

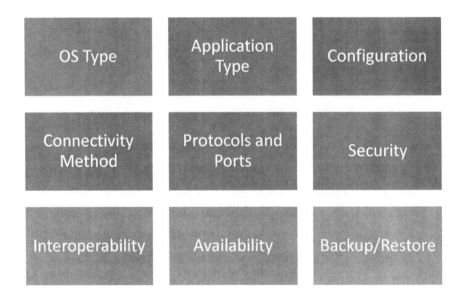

Figure 26 – Minimum Operating System and Software Requirements for Service

---

Services

In order to achieve standardization across infrastructure services, the outsourced service provider or internal service manager may consider the following and establish specific baseline requirements based upon the role of these services in supporting the infrastructure:

- Type of service (Telco, broadband, hosting, Co-Lo, remote backup/storage, etc.)
- Provider
- Specific configuration
- Service availability and redundancy
- Support/SLA
- Communication and status reporting
- Security methods
- Interoperability and ability to communicate with other local or remote systems, services, functions
- Service availability and redundancy
- Service backup, restore and business continuity processes

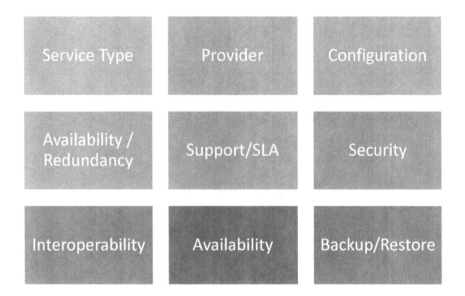

Figure 27 – Minimum Operating System and Software Requirements for Service

For a Microsoft Windows-centric environment, the outsourced service provider or internal service manager may establish the following baseline requirements for service:

- All Servers with Microsoft Windows Operating Systems must be running Windows 2008 Server or later, and have all of the latest Microsoft Service Packs and Critical Updates installed
- All Desktop PC's and notebooks/laptops with Microsoft Windows operating systems must be running Windows

---

7 or later, and have all of the latest Microsoft service packs and critical updates installed

- All Server and Desktop Software must be genuine, licensed and vendor-supported
- The environment must have a currently licensed, up-to-date and vendor-supported server-based antivirus solution protecting all servers, desktops, notebooks/laptops, and email
- The environment must have a currently licensed, vendor-supported server-based backup solution
- The environment must have a currently licensed, vendor-supported hardware firewall between the internal network and the Internet
- Any Wireless data traffic in the environment must be secured with a minimum of 128bit data encryption

These minimum requirements serve as examples only. Ultimately; and based on a variety of factors including internal capabilities, service deliverables and target market or client, it will be up to the outsourced service provider or internal service manager to determine the minimum environmental standards they will require in order to qualify for their services.

On-Boarding Clients

The Importance of an Effective On-Boarding Process
Once the decision has been made to begin service delivery for a new client, the outsourced service provider or internal service manager must execute an effective, efficient on-boarding process in order to meet client and end user expectations and facilitate future service.

A poorly designed and executed on-boarding process will quickly erode client and end user confidence and satisfaction and increase service delivery difficulty and cost for the outsourced service provider or internal service manager. No matter how you slice it, this is not the way to begin a new client relationship.

A successful on-boarding process begins before the decision is made to deliver services to the client.

Read that again. Now think about this – it is not possible to on-board a client successfully if the outsourced service provider or internal service manager does not collect the required data in order to set up the client's account and configure the Remote Monitoring and Management tool, Professional Services Automation solution, billing and communications systems to support them.

Some of this data-gathering occurs during the initial business needs analysis meeting with the client, and more is collected during the technology assessment of their infrastructure during the pre-sales process. Of course, once the decision has been made to deliver services to the client, more information is gathered in order to complete the collection of data required to properly on-board the client.

The Business Needs Analysis
Early in the client relationship; and during the pre-sales process, the outsourced service provider or internal service manager will conduct a business needs analysis with the prospect to gather the initial background information required to determine whether their support needs can be met, and if continuing to explore the feasibility of building a business relationship with them makes sense.

During this phase of the relationship, high-level information will be collected regarding the prospect's infrastructure including hardware, operating systems, application software, services and vendors. In addition, the prospect's business processes and workflows will be discussed and understood, as well as their growth plans and business goals, along with their bottlenecks and pain.

This information, along with office and branch office location and key staff, role and contact information will be gathered in

---

preparation for the technology assessment that must be conducted, should the decision to move forward be made.

The Technology Assessment

The technology assessment is the next step in gathering more granular data regarding the prospect's infrastructure in order to document and evaluate the hardware, operating systems, application software and services utilized in the environment, as well as their operating state and role in supporting the prospect's business processes.

The outsourced service provider or internal service manager will leverage their chosen tools and technology; including the Remote Monitoring and Management tool, in order to automate as much of the discovery and data-gathering process during the technology assessment phase as possible, and evaluate the resultant output to qualify the infrastructure's suitability for services.

Required Infrastructure Modifications, Updates and Upgrades

Once the results of the technology assessment have been collated, the outsourced service provider or internal service manager can compare the data against their established minimum requirements to determine what modifications, updates or upgrades will need to be performed in order to qualify the environment for services.

After the required infrastructure modifications, updates and upgrades have been completed, client on-boarding can commence.

The Provisioning Process
In this scenario, the client provisioning process is typically characterized as those processes and procedures required to prepare the client, their end users and infrastructure to receive and participate in the outsourced service provider's or internal service manager's NOC and Service Desk services, and may include collecting all of the data required, and conducting the following activities:

- Set up the client's account in the outsourced service provider's or internal service manager's Remote Monitoring and Management tool, Professional Services Automation solution, Communication and billing solutions, including all required supported user information
- If the Remote Monitoring and Management tool is appliance-based, configure and deploy the appliance per manufacturer or vendor recommendations for secure communications to and from the end user or client location and the outsourced service provider's or internal service manager's NOC, Datacenter or Service Desk

---

- If the Remote Monitoring and Management tool is agent-based, configure and deploy agents as required to monitor managed devices, operating systems, software applications and services per manufacturer or vendor recommendations and enable secure Remote Access and Control and communications to and from the end user or client location and the outsourced service provider's or internal service manager's NOC, Datacenter or Service Desk
- If applicable, initialize a discovery routine by the Remote Monitoring and Management tool to identify all network-connected devices and their roles in the environment, or use other means to capture this information and document it in the RMM tool and Professional Services Automation solution
- Associate the applicable Remote Monitoring and Management tool's default monitoring templates to all managed devices, operating systems, software applications and services
- Develop base monitoring templates and assign them to all devices, operating systems, software applications and services which the Remote Monitoring and Management tool did not identify or does not have a default template for
- Configure, test and confirm end user's or client's ability to generate properly formatted service requests

with all required information via email and the
Professional Services Automation solution's Service
Desk portal

- Test and confirm proper two-way communications and
  alerting to and from managed devices, operating
  systems, software applications and services at the end
  user or client location and the outsourced service
  provider's or internal service manager's NOC,
  Datacenter or Service Desk
- Configure, test and confirm proper operation of the
  Remote Monitoring and Management tool's Remote
  Access and Control function for managed devices and
  operating systems
- Configure, test and confirm proper two-way
  integration with the Remote Monitoring and
  Management tool; with raised alerts resulting in
  properly formatted service request generation
  including end user, device and client identification
  information included, as well as correct status
  updating and alert cancellation occurring in the
  Remote Monitoring and Management tool upon
  service request resolution in the Professional Services
  Automation solution
- Configure, test and confirm proper scripting and
  deployment of unattended operating system and

---

supported software application patches and updates by the RMM tool
- Configure, test and confirm proper scripting and execution of unattended device and operating system optimization activities such as deletion of temporary files and disk defragmentation by RMM tool
- Customize client reports in Professional Services Automation solution and test
- Configure, test and confirm proper report generation and automated report delivery by the PSA solution

Key infrastructure information required by the outsourced service provider or internal service manager for provisioning may include:

- Client contact information
- Server(s) information (type, make/model, role, warranty, support, OS, version, configuration, etc.)
- Server application information (type, role, warranty, support, version, configuration, licensing, etc.)
- Server services configuration information (IIS, DNS, DHCP, file & print, line of business, etc.)
- Internal Active Directory information (AD Domain, administrator account, users and computers, etc.)
- Network shares, security and distribution groups, etc.

- Line of business application information (type, role, warranty, support, version, configuration, licensing, etc.)
- LAN and WAN information (devices, configuration, addressing, protocols, security, etc.)
- External Domain Registration information (provider, account, domain name, registrar, DNS, expiration, etc.)
- ISP information (provider, account, configuration, expiration, etc.)
- Web and email hosting information (provider, account, configuration, expiration, etc.)
- Router, Switch, Firewall information (type, make/model, configuration, addressing, support, warranty, etc.)
- Anti-virus, Anti-spam and Anti-spyware information (type, vendor, role, warranty, support, version, configuration, licensing, etc.)
- Backup, Disaster Recovery and Business Continuity information (configuration, processes, etc.)
- Workstation, laptop and Smartphone information (type, role, warranty, support, version, configuration, etc.)
- Application and productivity software information (type, role, warranty, support, version, configuration, etc.)

- Printer, POS and peripheral information (network scanners, faxes, document imaging solutions, credit card terminals, etc.)
- Other network-attached device information (type, product, service, role, account, warranty, support, etc.)
- Vendor information (type, product, service, role, account, warranty, support, etc.)

This information and more must be collected and archived in the outsourced service provider's or internal service manager's Professional Services Automation solution in order to provide the NOC and Service Desk all of the information necessary to deliver services to the client in one managed location.

The Training Process

Prior to service turn-up or go-live, the outsourced service provider or internal service manager's NOC and Service Desk staff, as well as the new client and their end users need to be trained.

NOC and Service Desk Client Support Training

Prior to service turn-up or go-live, the outsourced service provider's or internal service manager's NOC and Service Desk teams must become familiar with the new client's infrastructure and its specific support requirements, along with any required modifications to established support processes for this particular client or their end users, such as communication, escalation or status reporting processes.

Client and End User Support Training

Prior to service turn-up or go-live, the outsourced service provider or internal service manager will typically conduct a training or multiple training sessions to indoctrinate the client and their end users on their NOC and Service Desk's processes and procedures for service delivery, and set the appropriate expectations in regards to response and incident management. Topics that may be covered during client and end user training may include:

- How to open a service request (email, portal, phone, etc.)
- Service Desk processes (incident, problem, configuration, change, risk, communication, release, service level, availability, capacity, service continuity, security, communication management, etc.)
- Service Desk response and incident management-specific processes (issue identification, documentation, prioritization, assignment, remediation, escalation, completion, QA, closure, communication, etc.)
- Support tiers
- Service Level Agreement
- Customer Service
- Reporting

Service Go-Live

After the outsourced service provider or internal service manager's NOC and Service Desk has completed their client-specific training and the client and their end users have received their support training, a service turn-up, or go-live date can be established. This is the date that all systems, processes, services, NOC and Service Desk staff and the client and their infrastructure and end users will be designated as ready to participate in NOC and Service Desk maintenance and support services.

The first thirty days after go-live with a new client will be the most critical for the outsourced service provider or internal service manager and their staff, as this is the time when the end users will be the most critical, and need to be won over by the new support relationship and its service delivery processes. If there are too many hiccups during this sensitive period, it may be difficult to recover the relationship. This is why it is imperative that the entire on-boarding process run smoothly, all processes are tested and validated, all required information is collected and documented in the Professional Services Automation solution and NOC and Service Desk staff and the client and their end users complete their individual on-boarding training prior to the decision to go live with the outsourced service provider's or internal service manager's support services.

Delivering Service

Day to Day Service Delivery

Although many of the roles, processes, procedures, activities and responsibilities of an outsourced service provider's or internal service manager's NOC and Service Desk and their respective personnel are more alike than they are dissimilar, once again, the differentiator between the two is the focus of their responsibilities.

Although the NOC's duties and responsibilities are oriented towards proactively managing and maintaining efficient operating states of hardware devices, software operating systems and applications and insuring the continuity of services; and the Service Desk's and its staff's duties and responsibilities are focused on managing end user incidents and problems, they both respond to incidents and problems that impact these by following established service delivery processes.

Based on best practices for proactive and reactive maintenance and service delivery, at a high level, the general framework governing these processes is shared by both the NOC and Service Desk, with differences surfacing based upon specific tasks. The following sections will reflect this similarity at a high level.

The NOC Staff's Daily Duties

The NOC staff's daily duties are determined by the outsourced service provider's, or internal service manager's NOC manager, whose responsibility includes the management of the NOC, and the proper identification, prioritization and assignment of all alerts/service requests and proactive maintenance duties to the appropriate queue, tier or resource.

In this context, and since the outsourced service provider's or internal service manager's Remote Monitoring and Management tool's alerts generate service requests in the Professional Services Automation solution, the NOC staff's typical day may resemble the following:

- Log in to the outsourced service provider's or internal service manager's Professional Services Automation solution
- Review all newly-assigned service requests to him/her
- Review any service requests previously assigned and still open to insure they are not in danger of falling outside of SLA (service dispatcher and/or NOC manager should be alerted to this status automatically by the PSA solution before it occurs)
- Work service requests in order of priority
  - Accept service request and time stamp
  - Review service request

- o Consult information documented in PSA solution as needed in order to perform incident management
- o Qualify issue to determine if it can be resolved through tier 1 support within SLA
- o Work issue to successful resolution
- o Verify issue to be resolved
- o Document complete incident resolution details in PSA solution, mark status complete and time stamp
- o Service request is placed in 24 hour QA status for monitoring
- o Service request is closed once issue is determined to be resolved
- If service request cannot be resolved through tier 1 support, or is in danger of falling outside of SLA:
  - o Service Request is escalated to Tier 2 and successive tiers of support in accordance with outsourced service provider's or internal service manager's service delivery process

All proactive maintenance activity is also scheduled, assigned and managed in the outsourced service provider's or internal service manager's Professional Services Automation solution. Additional duties carried out by NOC staff may include:

- Review of monitoring reports to identify issues or trends that may impact service or business process continuity for clients or end users in order to

---

address them in advance of potential interruption; or for capacity planning purposes

- Script or manually deliver required hardware, operating system, application software or service updates, patches and hotfixes
- Assist in new client on-boarding activities
- Customize, produce and deliver performance reports to internal NOC management
- Modify and tune alerting and thresholds on monitored devices, operating systems, application software and services in order to improve effectiveness and efficiency
- Manage, maintain and update internal and client and end user infrastructure documentation, processes and procedures in PSA solution

The Service Desk Staff's Daily Duties

The Service Desk staff's daily duties are determined by the outsourced service provider's, or internal service manager's Service Desk manager, whose responsibility includes the management of the Service Desk, and the proper prioritization and assignment of all service requests to the appropriate tier. The scheduling of all service work is ultimately the responsibility of the Service Desk manager, but this and other functions may be performed by a service dispatcher. It is the Service Desk manager's ultimate responsibility to make certain the Service Desk maintains their SLAs.

In this context, a Service Desk staff's typical day may resemble the following:

- Log in to the outsourced service provider's or internal service manager's Professional Services Automation solution
- Review all newly-assigned service requests to him/her
- Review any service requests previously assigned and still open to insure they are not in danger of falling outside of SLA (service dispatcher and/or Service Desk manager should be alerted to this status automatically by the PSA solution before it occurs)
- Work service requests in order of priority
    - Accept service request and time stamp
    - Review service request
    - Contact client or end user as needed to gather any additional information necessary in order to begin incident management
    - Consult information documented in PSA solution as needed in order to perform incident management
    - Qualify issue to determine if it can be resolved through tier 1 support within SLA
    - Work issue to successful resolution
    - Verify issue to be resolved to end user's satisfaction
    - Document complete incident resolution details in PSA solution, mark status complete and time stamp

---

- o Service request is placed in 24 hour QA status, after which the end user is contacted to verify the issue has been resolved to their satisfaction and asked if the service request can be closed
  - o Service request is closed
- If service request cannot be resolved through tier 1 support, or is in danger of falling outside of SLA:
  - o Service Request is escalated to Tier 2 and successive tiers of support in accordance with outsourced service provider's or internal service manager's service delivery process

As with NOC staff, Service Desk staff will also have additional duties to carry out, which may include:

- Review of Service Desk reports to identify end user or equipment issues or trends that may impact customer satisfaction or service or business process continuity for clients or end users in order to proactively address them
- Assist in new client on-boarding activities
- Customize, produce and deliver performance reports to internal Service Desk management
- Manage, maintain and update internal and client and end user infrastructure documentation, processes and procedures in PSA solution

Interacting with Clients and End Users

Again, because of the reality that Service Desk services are typically delivered remotely; and end users, clients and the outsourced service provider's or internal service manager's staff may never have the opportunity to physically meet each other, it is critical for the outsourced service provider's or internal service manager's staff to excel at interpersonal communications in all forms with clients, and especially verbal communications with them over the phone.

Adhering to the outsourced service provider's or internal service manager's established communication protocols will assist in reflecting a professional, courteous, efficient image for end users and clients, fostering trust, loyalty and customer satisfaction over time. The following are some additional tips for Service Desk staff to consider when communicating verbally with end users or clients.

What To Say, What Not To Say, and How Not To Say It

Being human like the rest of us, the outsourced service provider's or internal service manager's staff will find themselves in situations when speaking with a client or end user where they might say too much, or say the wrong thing, or say the right thing in the wrong way, or say the right thing, but in doing so contradict something that the client or end user had been told previously by someone else. In any of these scenarios, a top-of-mind awareness and fear of accidentally doing any of these things during conversations with clients or end users is required by all Service Desk staff. Here are some things to keep in mind:

- **Be courteous and professional and ask questions pertaining to the issue at hand** – steer clear of idle chit-chat and volunteering too much personal information like what the Service Desk staff did over the weekend, last night, or inquiring the same of the client or end user. This will help keep the relationship in the proper perspective

- **Refrain from volunteering potential causes of the issue, or "thinking out loud"** – when the issue turns out not to be caused by the Service Desk staff's overheard suspicions, it may erode the perception of their competence by the client or end user

- **Do not have internal discussions with other staff members on an open line** – even though one Service Desk staff is handling their call professionally and following communication protocol, others may fail to do so in open conversation

- **Use the hold or mute button constantly** – this is the safest way to insure the client or end user is prevented from hearing the wrong thing, and allows the Service Desk staff to focus on resolving the incident as quickly as possible without distraction. Using mute allows the

Service Desk staff to monitor the line, should the client or end user wish to volunteer any useful information, or check status

- **Blank the end user's desktop during remote control sessions whenever possible** – this practice helps reduce questions during the troubleshooting process, and the potential perception by the client or end user that the Service Desk staff isn't competent because they are investigating so many different things during the troubleshooting session
- **Don't tell the client or end user what you did** – the more information is shared with the client or end user, the more of that information can be misinterpreted, misunderstood, or again, contradict what they were told by someone else. Here is a great example of how to handle a call with an end user following all of these bullet points:

Example Service Request Call:

Service Desk staff: Hi, Mary – this is Bob from the Service Desk. I'm calling you to follow up on the service request you opened regarding "X" – is this a good time for me to troubleshoot that with you?

Mary: Hi Bob, yes this is a good time.

Service Desk staff: Great, my understanding from reading the service request notes is that ………………….. Is that correct?

Mary: Yes Bob – that's what is happening.

Service Desk staff: Okay, do you mind if I start a remote desktop sharing session with you, so I can begin troubleshooting?

Mary: Sure Bob, go right ahead.

Service Desk staff: Okay, Mary – I'm going to put you on mute while the session initiates, and pick back up when I'm connected. Will that be okay?

Mary: No problem, Bob.

Service Desk staff places end user on mute while session is initiated

Service Desk staff: Okay, Mary – I'm in. Would it be ok if I take a look at a few things in order to help narrow down the cause of the issue? I'll need to blank your screen while I do so – is that also ok?

Mary: Sure, do whatever you need, Bob.

Service Desk staff: Thanks, Mary. I'm also going to place you on mute for about five minutes while I troubleshoot. Would

---

that be ok? You can feel free to take a short break or grab a coffee or water...can I see you back in five?

Mary: Ok

Service Desk staff performs incident management

After five minutes:

Service Desk staff: Hi Mary – I can hear that you're back – are you with me?

Mary: Yes Bob, I'm here.

Service Desk staff: Great. I think I may have discovered the cause of the issue, and I've made a few changes that I think will resolve it. Is it ok with you if I place this service request in a QA status for 24 hours, and our team follows up with you tomorrow to make sure it's resolved before we close this service request?

Mary: Sure, Bob. Thank you for your help. What was the problem? What did you do?

Service Desk staff: You're welcome, Mary – it was my pleasure. Until I'm 100% confident that the issue is resolved, I prefer to keep from stating with absolute certainty what the cause was and the fix – *you know, I could be wrong! (jokingly)* How about we wait for the QA process so I can be sure, and if

---

---

you're still interested, we'll be happy to share the technical details with you. Is that ok?

Mary: Oh sure, Bob, it's really not that important.

Service Desk staff: Ok then, Mary, I'll document our support session in the notes here and place this request in our QA queue for 24 hours. If the issue should happen to crop up again, please let us know, ok?

Mary: Sure will. Thanks again.

Service Desk staff: My pleasure. Have a great day.

Can you appreciate how smoothly this support session went? I'll bet you were wondering just how in the world a Service Desk staff could effectively deliver a support session by blanking the user's desktop (of course this won't be possible in all cases), placing the end user on mute for most of it, and then not sharing what the cause of the issue was, or even better – what they did to resolve it.

Now, if the issue does recur, and a different Service Desk staff is assigned to work on it, there is no potential for the end user to complicate the session with misheard or misinterpreted data from the first support session. And because the service request wasn't closed, but instead placed in a QA status, with the end user's expectations set appropriately, the Service Desk staff has avoided the "you didn't fix it the first time" or "this is the second (or third) time I've opened a request for the same thing" perception, as the issue was never considered resolved and the request was never closed.

Client Satisfaction

Measuring Client Satisfaction and Improving Retention
If the outsourced service provider or internal service manager does not develop and execute a consistent, effective process to measure client and end user satisfaction in order to institute a continual client satisfaction improvement process, they will be doing their clients, end users and NOC and Service Desk staff a disservice.

The only way to realize improvement in any endeavor is to measure performance. Just as important as it is to measure performance of the NOC and Service Desk against SLA and other key performance metrics in order to establish a baseline and work towards improvement, it is even more important to measure client satisfaction.

It does the outsourced service provider or internal service manager absolutely no good whatsoever to believe they have the best processes and procedures for service delivery in place, but have no way to measure their client's or end user's satisfaction, and risk losing them for unknown reasons.

The best way to gauge a decision maker's satisfaction is face to face during regular strategic meetings. It is important to set aside time specifically for measuring the client's satisfaction, preferably at the beginning of these meetings. The outsourced service provider or internal service manager will want to know the client's feedback on their performance, and may ask questions such as:

- "On a scale of one to five, what is your overall satisfaction level with our services?"
- "Can you share with me why you rated us that way, and what we can do to improve your overall satisfaction?" Or "Are there specific areas that we can improve on to raise your overall satisfaction level with our services?"
- "How would you rate your satisfaction level with our customer service?"
- "How would you rate the overall quality of our strategic business relationship?"
- "How would you rate your level of satisfaction with the value of our services?"
- "How likely would it be for you to recommend our services to another organization or business acquaintance?"

The best way to gauge end user satisfaction may be through anonymous survey, and if possible, delivered via phone by an outside 3rd-party organization. End users tend to elaborate more when answering survey questions verbally, as the surveyor can drill deeper into the answers offered by the end user respondent.

Other ways to gauge end user satisfaction are through electronic surveys, which can also be completed anonymously. Some Professional Services Automation solutions support survey creation natively and enable both automatic and scheduled survey delivery and response reporting. Caution – if a standard service request survey is delivered in an automated fashion after every service request closure, end users will eventually cease responding to them. This is why it is important to create and deliver surveys purposefully and periodically to receive the greatest response, and vary the questions from survey to survey to maintain interest in the respondent.

Surveys delivered in this fashion must be clear and specific in their intent. For instance, is the survey gauging overall satisfaction, or satisfaction from services received from a specific tier, queue or individual staff member? Surveys must also be simple to understand and easy to respond to. Keep questions short – one sentence; if possible, and clear. If the respondent has to figure out what the question means, the value of their feedback will be diminished, as each respondent will comprehend the question differently and skew the results.

The outsourced service provider or internal service manager should keep each survey brief – end users should perceive it to take only a few minutes at most to complete a survey to increase response – 5 to 10 questions at the most, if they are simply gauging satisfaction.

The outsourced service provider or internal service manager should be prepared to act on the survey responses received. Taking the time to develop and deliver surveys and collate responses without an action plan to execute on to raise client and end user satisfaction is pointless.

Sample electronic end user satisfaction survey questions may resemble:

- On a scale of 1 through 5, with 5 being highest, please rate your overall level of satisfaction with the Service Desk
- On a scale of 1 through 5, with 5 being highest, please rate your level of satisfaction with the Service Desk's response time
- On a scale of 1 through 5, with 5 being highest, please rate your level of satisfaction with the Service Desk's resolution time
- On a scale of 1 through 5, with 5 being highest, please rate your level of satisfaction with the Service Desk's customer service
- On a scale of 1 through 5, with 5 being highest, please rate your level of satisfaction with the Service Desk's communications

Client Satisfaction

- On a scale of 1 through 5, with 5 being highest, please rate your level of satisfaction with the Service Desk's performance in keeping your systems up and running

These survey questions are included as an example only. The outsourced service provider or internal service manager should carefully determine the areas of satisfaction they would like end user feedback on and create short, easy to understand surveys whose questions are clear and concise, with a numeric rating system for each question in order to facilitate analysis in a meaningful way – then act on the results and measure improvement over time through additional surveys.

Section 6 – Hiring and Training Technical Staff

The following chapters will cover effective means for writing employment ads that attract the right talent, using DISC behavioral profiles before interviewing prospective NOC and Service Desk staff to make certain the outsourced service provider or internal service manager is interviewing the right candidates, how to interview these candidates and which questions to ask, along with creating an offer letter and employment agreement and developing a compensation plan and training requirements.

Writing Effective Employment Ads for Technical Staff

Writing an employment ad for technical staff may be the first HR act an outsourced service provider or internal service manager performs in the search for talent. Let's take a moment to understand the motivating factors behind technically-oriented people. Technical staff's ideal work environment may include challenging technical work, ongoing training opportunities and a team approach to problem solving and solution design and delivery, along with appreciation and respect for their contributions to the team; with high monetary incentives ranking lower on the list of requirements when seeking employment, or in their decision to remain with their current employer. Technicians' behavior normally falls into the Coordinator/ Supporter/ Relater areas of a DISC (behavioral) profile. A DISC profile is a psychometric testing technique that uses a simple questionnaire as a basis for revealing insights into a person's normal, adapted and work behaviors, and we will explore utilizing DISC profiles to our advantage during the hiring process in the next chapter.

Understanding these motivators for technical staff, effective employment ads highlight these specific areas in the body of the advertisement. The ad copy writer's job is to effectively promote the employment opportunity to the best technicians available. The outsourced service provider or internal service manager is not looking for anybody that can fog a mirror – they want seasoned technicians and engineers, whose past performance is an indicator of their future potential.

A good new technical hire will dive right in to learning every last detail about the outsourced service provider's or internal service manager's NOC and Service Desk, and take it seriously to become a subject matter expert on everything they support. There is a clear pecking order with them, and their respect is earned by knowing more than they do about a particular subject. These are the type of individuals that jump right in to their positions soon after they are hired, and suck up information like a dry sponge.

Technicians and engineers see things as black and white problems to solve without a lot of emotion, and the really good ones can build personal relationships with clients and end users and understand that their job is to build rapport with them to establish the trust necessary to elevate the outsourced service provider's or internal service manager's NOC or Service Desk's overall perception as that of a valuable resource that can solve their technical problems and identify solutions to increase their efficiencies, productivity and mitigate their business pain and risk.

Writing Effective Employment Ads for Technical Staff

These behavioral traits are what to look for in technical staff. It can be difficult to find the right staff with the right mix of technical capability, customer service and desire to do the job right the first time.

But first things first – before the outsourced service provider or internal service manager has the ability to start the DISC profiling and interview process, they need candidates. And to get candidates interested in their employment opportunity they need to write compelling employment ads.

So they need to structure the employment ad to cover the basics, plus highlight the nuances that will attract the technical professionals they seek. In the old days (pre-Internet), it was necessary to excel at "classified ad shorthand" for print ads in the employment section of newspapers. This was the process where the ad copy writer would try to condense full words enough to save on the cost of the ad, while still conveying the gist of their message. Now the luxury of posting just about any size ad through online job sites such as Monster, Careerbuilder, Dice, Hotjobs and others for a reasonable fee, in addition to having it run for months at a time, greatly improves the process and results. Let's look at the basic components of an employment posting for a Service Desk position:

Company name and location
Job status – Full Time, Employee
Relevant Work Experience – 3 years minimum
Job Category – Service Desk
Career Level – Experienced

Job Description – Several short paragraphs documenting the desired candidate's qualities, the position's responsibilities and job duties (emphasis on challenging technical work, ongoing training opportunities and a team approach to problem solving)

Minimum Skills Required – A short bulleted list of required skills and experience

Benefits – A short paragraph detailing salary range, bonuses and other benefits

A method of contacting the company

Okay, now let's take a look at a representative employment ad that conforms to many of the points in the above layout:

Company: MSP University
Location: Garden Grove, CA 92841
Status: Full-Time, Employee
Job Category: Service Desk
Relevant Work Experience: 3-5 Years
Career Level: Experienced (Non-Manager)

We are currently seeking a highly skilled Service Desk representative with the drive and determination to help us support our client base. This position reports to our service manager. We are looking for an individual who is a problem-solver and has a proven track record of working within a team environment to successfully address challenging user computing issues, and is accustomed to leveraging technical training opportunities to improve their skills. If you have the experience and the desire, we'd like to talk to you.

Our Service Desk representatives are responsible for maintaining user uptime and improving their computing experiences through effective remote monitoring, maintenance and problem identification and resolution activities, as well as growing and developing the organization's perception with existing clients through exceptional customer service. Candidates must be energetic and focused with a strong motivation to learn new technologies and management and maintenance processes. This position requires dedication, persistence, follow-up, effective utilization of provided resources and unbeatable customer service.

This position will include identifying user problems and working within a structured problem management and resolution process to remediate issues within established SLAs, and involves working with other resources and vendors to deliver effective support services. Responsibilities include identifying, documenting and troubleshooting user computing issues to resolution and maintaining client satisfaction.

Job duties include utilizing our remote monitoring and management (RMM) and professional services automation (PSA) solutions along with other service-specific tools and technologies to deliver remote user support services and update service request information, answer technical support calls, assign ticket severity, prioritize work accordingly, and collaborate and work with other staff and vendor support resources to resolve issues. Overall relationship management and the ability to coordinate required resources to respond to complex IT requirements is desired. Other requirements include participating in ongoing training and attainment of manufacturer certifications, developing and maintaining relationships with user and vendor contacts, and preparing and presenting service and monitoring reports to management regularly.

Minimum skills required:

- Minimum three years Service Desk experience
- Microsoft Certified Professional status
- Excellent knowledge of Microsoft software and technologies
- Strong interpersonal skills required to effectively communicate with users and vendors

- Passion for teamwork, continuing education, problem solving and exceptional customer service
- Must be well spoken, outgoing, organized, detailed-orientated, dependable and flexible
- Experience with HP, Cisco and Citrix technologies a plus
- Valid driver's license and proof of insurance
- Background check and drug screen required
- Reliable transportation

This position entails:

- Troubleshooting user problems over the phone and with remote control technologies
- Accurate documentation of all activities conducted
- The ability to manage, maintain, troubleshoot and support our users' networks, equipment, software and services
- The ability to learn quickly and adapt to changing requirements

The successful candidate must be:

- Professional and articulate
- Interpersonally adept
- Technically proficient
- A relationship builder
- A problem solver

Benefits include group medical/dental insurance, paid vacation, holidays, personal & sick time and training reimbursement. Our generous compensation plans are structured as salary plus bonuses for meeting utilization, compliance and customer service requirements, with initial compensation commensurate with relevant experience.

Qualified candidates please submit a current resume, along with salary history to: hr@mspu.us.

Resources

Careerbuilder.com
www.careerbuilder.com

Dice.com
www.dice.com

Hotjobs.com
www.hotjobs.com

Monster.com
www.monster.com

Using DISC Behavioral Profiles Before Interviewing Candidates

I remember clearly how hit-and-miss our success at hiring the right staff used to be before we discovered the value of utilizing DISC behavioral profiling in our hiring process. Based upon the groundbreaking work of William Moulton Marston Ph.D. (1893 - 1947) in the (then) emerging field of psychology, DISC measures four dimensions of normal human behavior:

- **Dominance** - relating to control, power and assertiveness (how we respond to problems or challenges)
- **Influence** - relating to social situations and communication (how we influence others to our point of view)
- **Steadiness** (submission in Marston's time) - relating to patience, persistence, and thoughtfulness (how we respond to the pace of our environment)
- **Conscientiousness** (or caution, compliance in Marston's time) - relating to structure and organization (how we respond to rules and procedures set by others)

We have not only been able to significantly improve our success rate at hiring the right staff since implementing DISC profiling, but we have used DISC profiles to help in team-building efforts. If you haven't read Jim Collins' excellent book "Good to Great", do yourself a favor and pick up a copy. One of the key concepts in "Good to Great" is that of not only "getting the right people on the bus", but "getting the right people in the right seats on the bus". DISC behavioral profiles help us achieve both of these objectives.

Based upon answering a series of twenty-four questions, each with the directive to choose what a candidate is "most like" and "least like", the DISC profile will generate a voluminous report describing the subject's behavior with incredible accuracy. Here is a representative example of the types of questions a subject is asked to answer in a DISC profile:

Each question has two answers – choose one answer that indicates which you are **Most Like**, and one answer that indicates which you are **Least Like**. Each question requires two choices:

Using DISC Behavioral Profiles Before Interviewing Candidates

Most Like	Least Like	
		Gentle, kindly
		Persuasive, convincing
	x	Humble, reserved, modest
x		Original, inventive, individualistic

		Attractive, Charming, attracts others
x		Cooperative, agreeable
		Stubborn, unyielding
	x	Sweet, pleasing

	x	Easily led, follower
x		Bold, daring
		Loyal, faithful, devoted
		Charming, delightful

Using DISC Behavioral Profiles Before Interviewing Candidates

It seems almost unbelievable that merely completing twenty-four questions like this can create a comprehensive behavioral profile that we have come to rely on in each and every one of our hiring decisions. And I've got to admit that when we have gone ahead and made a hiring decision in spite of some red flags uncovered by a DISC profile, we've always come to regret it.

Here's a sample portion of a fictitious DISC profile:

Elizabeth prefers being a team player, and wants each player to contribute along with her. Many people see her as a self-starter dedicated to achieving results. She can be blunt and critical of people who do not meet her standards. She may have difficulty dealing with others who are slower in thought and action. Elizabeth has the ability to question people's basic assumptions about things. She prides herself on her creativity, incisiveness and cleverness. She can be incisive, analytical and argumentative at times. She is aggressive and confident. She tends to have a "short fuse" and can display anger or displeasure when she feels that people are taking advantage of her. Elizabeth is forward-looking, aggressive and competitive. His vision for results is one of her positive strengths. She is comfortable in an environment that may be characterized by high pressure and is variety-oriented.

Using DISC Behavioral Profiles Before Interviewing Candidates

---

Elizabeth will work long hours until a tough problem is solved. After it is solved, Elizabeth may become bored with any routine work that follows. She is logical, incisive and critical in her problem-solving activities. She sometimes gets so involved in a project that she tends to take charge. She usually takes time when confronted with a major decision; that is, she takes an unemotional approach to analyzing the data and facts. Others may see this as vacillating; however she is just thinking through all the ramifications of her decision. Elizabeth finds it easy to share her opinions on solving work-related problems. Sometimes she may be so opinionated about a particular problem that she has difficulty letting others participate in the process. She sometimes requires assistance in bringing major projects to completion. She may have so many projects underway that she needs help from others. She likes the freedom to explore and the authority to re-examine and retest her findings.

Elizabeth tends to be intolerant of people who seem ambiguous or think too slowly. She usually communicates in a cool and direct manner. Some may see her as being aloof and blunt. When communicating with others, Elizabeth must carefully avoid being excessively critical or pushy. She tries to get on with the subject, while others may be trying to work through the details. She is skilled at asking informed questions and extracting information, but for some people she may need to phrase her questions more tactfully. Her creative and active

---

mind may hinder her ability to communicate to others effectively. She may present the information in a form that cannot be easily understood by some people. Others often misunderstand her great ability as a creative thinker. She is not influenced by people who are overly enthusiastic. They rarely get her attention. She may display a lack of empathy for others who cannot achieve her standards.

Here are some other excerpts from Elizabeth's DISC Profile:

Value to the organization:

This section of the report identifies the specific talents and behavior Elizabeth brings to the job. By looking at these statements, one can identify her role in the organization. The organization can then develop a system to capitalize on her particular value and make her an integral part of the team.

- Thinks big
- Forward-looking and future-oriented
- Presents the facts without emotion
- Places high value on time
- Usually makes decisions with the bottom line in mind
- Innovative
- Always looking for logical solutions
- Initiates activity
- Challenge-oriented

Using DISC Behavioral Profiles Before Interviewing Candidates

---

Ideal environment:

This section identifies the ideal work environment based on Elizabeth's basic style. People with limited flexibility will find themselves uncomfortable working in any job not described in this section. People with flexibility use intelligence to modify their behavior and can be comfortable in many environments. Use this section to identify specific duties and responsibilities that Elizabeth enjoys and also those that create frustration.

- Evaluation based on results, not the process
- Non-routine work with challenge and opportunity
- An innovative and futuristic-oriented environment
- Projects that produce tangible results
- Data to analyze
- Private office or work area
- Environment where she can be a part of the team, but removed from office politics
- Forum to express ideas and viewpoints

Perceptions:

A person's behavior and feelings may be quickly telegraphed to others. This section provides additional information on Elizabeth's self-perception and how, under certain conditions, others may perceive her behavior. Understanding this section will empower Elizabeth to project the image that will allow her to control the situation.

Self-perception:

Elizabeth usually sees herself as being:

- Pioneering
- Assertive
- Competitive
- Confident
- Positive
- Winner

Other's perception:

Under moderate pressure, tension, stress or fatigue, others may see her as being:

- Demanding
- Nervy
- Egotistical
- Aggressive

And, under extreme pressure, stress or fatigue, others may see her as being:

- Abrasive
- Controlling
- Arbitrary
- Opinionated

Using DISC Behavioral Profiles Before Interviewing Candidates

Descriptors:

Based on Elizabeth's responses, the report has marked those words that describe her personal behavior. They describe how she solves problems and meets challenges, influences people, responds to the pace of the environment and how she responds to rules and procedures set by others.

Dominance	Influencing	Steadiness	Compliance
Demanding	Effusive	Phlegmatic	Evasive
Egocentric	Inspiring	Relaxed	Worrisome
Driving	Magnetic	Resistant to Change	Careful
Ambitious	Political	Nondemonstrative	Dependent
Pioneering	Enthusiastic	Passive	Cautious
Strong-Willed	Demonstrative		Conventional
Forceful	Persuasive	Patient	Exacting
Determined	Warm		Neat
Aggressive	Convincing	Possessive	
Competitive	Polished		Systematic
Decisive	Poised	Predictable	Diplomatic
Venturesome	Optimistic	Consistent	Accurate
		Deliberate	Tactful
Inquisitive	Trusting	Steady	Open-Minded
Responsible	Sociable	Stable	Balanced Judgment
Conservative	Reflective	Mobile	Firm
Calculating	Factual	Active	Independent
Cooperative	Calculating	Restless	Self-Willed
Hesitant	Skeptical	Alert	Stubborn
Low-Keyed		Variety-Oriented	
Unsure	Logical	Demonstrative	Obstinate
Undemanding	Undemonstrative		
Cautious	Suspicious	Impatient	Opinionated
	Matter-of-Fact	Pressure-Oriented	Unsystematic
Mild	Incisive	Eager	Self-Righteous
Agreeable		Flexible	Uninhibited
Modest	Pessimistic	Impulsive	Arbitrary
Peaceful	Moody	Impetuous	Unbending
Unobtrusive	Critical	Hypertense	Careless with Details

Using DISC Behavioral Profiles Before Interviewing Candidates

---

Adapted style:

Elizabeth sees her present work environment requiring her to exhibit the behavior listed on this page. If the following statements DO NOT sound job related, explore the reasons why she is adapting this behavior.

- Precise, analytical approach to work tasks
- Acting without precedent, and able to respond to change in daily work
- Sensitivity to existing rules and regulations
- Limited contact with people
- Disciplined, meticulous attention to order
- Having the ability to see the "big picture" as well as the small pieces of the puzzle
- Careful, thoughtful approach to decision making
- Quickly responding to crisis and change, with a strong desire for immediate results
- Anticipating and solving problems
- Persistence in job completion
- Dealing with a wide variety of work activities
- Calculation of risks before taking action
- Accurate adherence to high quality standards

Using DISC Behavioral Profiles Before Interviewing Candidates

---

Keys to motivating:

Elizabeth wants:

- Evaluation on not only the results achieved, but the quality of the work and the price she paid for performance
- Sincere appreciation for achievements--may interpret as manipulation if overdone
- To explore new ideas and authority to test her findings
- To be part of a quality-oriented work group
- Support staff to do detail work
- To know the agenda for the meeting
- New challenges and problems to solve
- Freedom from controls that restrict her creativity
- To be seen as a leader
- Prestige, position and titles so she can control the destiny of others
- Meetings that stay on the agenda, or reasons for changing the agenda

Keys to managing:

Elizabeth needs:

- To know results expected and to be evaluated on the results
- To adjust her intensity to match the situation
- To be more cooperative with other team members

Using DISC Behavioral Profiles Before Interviewing Candidates

- A program for pacing work and relaxing
- To analyze constructive criticism to see if it's true and how it may be impacting her career
- To display empathy for people who approach life differently than she does
- To understand that her tendency to tell it like it is may reduce performance rather than raise it with some people
- To understand her role on the team--either a team player or the leader
- To negotiate commitment face-to-face
- Appreciation of the feelings of others
- To be objective and listen when others volunteer constructive criticism
- The opportunity to ask questions to clarify or determine why

Areas for improvement:

In this area is a listing of possible limitations without regard to a specific job. Review with Elizabeth and cross out those limitations that do not apply. Highlight 1 to 3 limitations that are hindering her performance and develop an action plan to eliminate or reduce this hindrance.

Using DISC Behavioral Profiles Before Interviewing Candidates

---

Elizabeth has a tendency to:

- Have no concept of the problems that slower-moving people may have with her style
- Be inconsistent because of many stops, starts and ever-changing direction
- Set standards for herself and others so high that impossibility of the situation is common place
- Have difficulty finding balance between family and work
- Have trouble delegating--can't wait, so does it herself

I hope by now you can see how extremely valuable this tool is, and why we choose to include it as a requirement during our hiring process.

So how exactly do we use the DISC profile? Well, we will review all of the resumes that come in for a particular job posting, and then determine who our top candidates are. After this, we will conduct a quick phone interview with each candidate, and the ones that make it to the next cut will be emailed a link to take our DISC behavioral profile online. We then review the resultant report, and decide who to call in for in-person interviews.

For technical staff candidates, in addition to the standard DISC behavioral profile, we will also have them take a specialized

---

version of the DISC profile, called the Personal Talent Skills Inventory (PTSI). The PTSI is an objective analysis of the candidate's understanding of themselves, their strengths and their weaknesses. An individual's talents and personal skills are a fundamental and integral part of who they are. The PTSI describes what an individual "can do" in 23 capacities, or personal skills, related to the business environment.

The PTSI is designed to capture how people see themselves and the world around them. To do this, it measures a person from two perspectives, external and internal, and in six dimensions, three in each perspective.

External:

- Empathetic Outlook ⇒ Judgment of people
- Practical Thinking ⇒ Judgment of tasks
- Systems Judgment ⇒ Judgment of systems

Internal:

- Sense of Self ⇒ Judgment of being
- Role Awareness ⇒ Judgment of doing
- Self Direction ⇒ Judgment of becoming

The PTSI report provides a ranking of personal skills that describe an individual's potential for workplace performance by determining their capability in several areas. After

Using DISC Behavioral Profiles Before Interviewing Candidates

---

analyzing the clarity, bias and intensity of each of the six dimensions, one can begin to understand an individual's self view and world view, gaining true insight into the internal and external perspectives that affect superior performance.

Understanding problem-solving techniques, and the ability to implement them effectively during service delivery, is how we define a successful technical resource. We utilize the PTSI to identify a candidate's problem-solving strengths and weaknesses and their ability to perform these functions in the workplace.

The following is a sample of the results from a fictitious PTSI:

Using DISC Behavioral Profiles Before Interviewing Candidates

---

Name: Elizabeth

World View

This is how Elizabeth sees the world around her. This view measures her clarity and understanding of people, tasks and systems. It could also be looked at in terms of feeling, doing and thinking from an external standpoint. The statements below are based primarily on the 3 dimensions on the left side of the dimensional balance page and are in a random order.

- Elizabeth may benefit from improving her relationships with authority figures
- She needs an environment in which contributions are recognized, properly rewarded, and appreciated.
- She has the ability to become action-oriented in order to complete the task at hand
- She performs best in an atmosphere where there is an open exchange of ideas and where feedback is readily available.
- Elizabeth can be versatile and can adapt to different types of people and changing situations
- She may benefit from understanding the importance of interpersonal relationships
- She needs an atmosphere that has structure and a defined chain of command
- She understands how to deal with ideas, knowledge, and systems

---

- Elizabeth has the ability to use her people skills in order to relate to others

Self View

This is how Elizabeth sees herself. This view measures her clarity and understanding of herself, her roles in life and her direction for the future. The internal dimensions are a reflection of her from both personal and professional viewpoints. The statements below are based primarily on the 3 dimensions on the right side of the dimensional balance page and are in a random order.

- Elizabeth tends to use her internal awareness to achieve the desired outcome during the process of a role change
- She may apply her life planning skills for personal growth
- She has a grasp of her actual and potential accomplishments, life roles and activities
- She has achieved a moderate level of self-understanding
- Elizabeth believes that her own worth is based equally on her sense of self, her life roles, and growing as a person
- She may focus on gaining information to clearly envision herself in the future
- She could get into a comfort zone which could restrict her from developing or applying more of her potential

- She tends to have a balanced understanding of herself, her roles and her future development
- Elizabeth tends to be adaptable, depending on what is called for in the current situation

As you can tell, this portion of the PTSI provides a good understanding of a candidate's perceptions of not only external environments such as the workplace, but of themselves as well, and can also be utilized as a tool to improve an existing technical candidate's skills or interpersonal relationships with others. The following section illustrates the PTSI's findings of a candidate's critical success skills in a visually appealing manner, and ranks the candidate's responses against the population:

Using DISC Behavioral Profiles Before Interviewing Candidates

Critical Success Skills

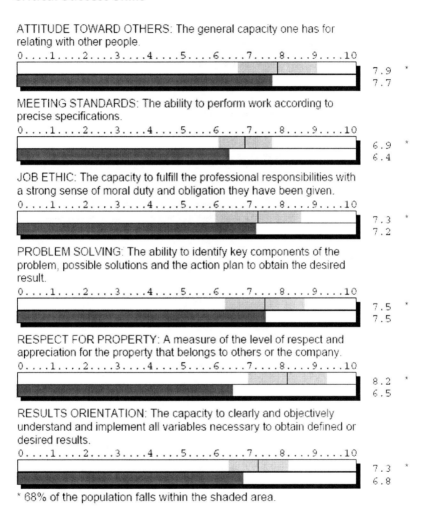

ATTITUDE TOWARD OTHERS: The general capacity one has for relating with other people.

```
0....1....2....3....4....5....6....7....8....9....10
```
7.9 *
7.7

MEETING STANDARDS: The ability to perform work according to precise specifications.

```
0....1....2....3....4....5....6....7....8....9....10
```
6.9 *
6.4

JOB ETHIC: The capacity to fulfill the professional responsibilities with a strong sense of moral duty and obligation they have been given.

```
0....1....2....3....4....5....6....7....8....9....10
```
7.3 *
7.2

PROBLEM SOLVING: The ability to identify key components of the problem, possible solutions and the action plan to obtain the desired result.

```
0....1....2....3....4....5....6....7....8....9....10
```
7.5 *
7.5

RESPECT FOR PROPERTY: A measure of the level of respect and appreciation for the property that belongs to others or the company.

```
0....1....2....3....4....5....6....7....8....9....10
```
8.2 *
6.5

RESULTS ORIENTATION: The capacity to clearly and objectively understand and implement all variables necessary to obtain defined or desired results.

```
0....1....2....3....4....5....6....7....8....9....10
```
7.3 *
6.8

* 68% of the population falls within the shaded area.

Using DISC Behavioral Profiles Before Interviewing Candidates

---

The General Employment Skills Summary

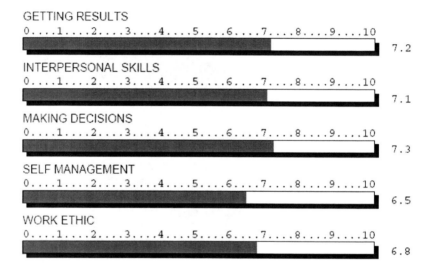

Using DISC Behavioral Profiles Before Interviewing Candidates

Getting Results

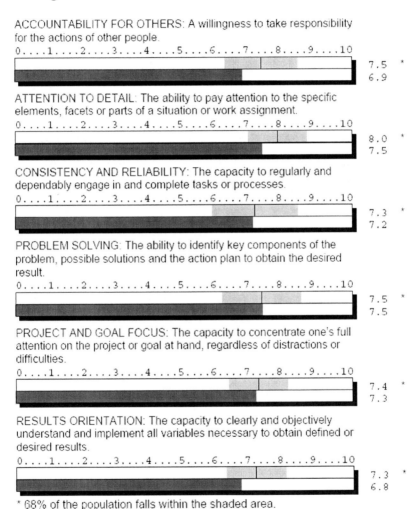

ACCOUNTABILITY FOR OTHERS: A willingness to take responsibility for the actions of other people.

0....1....2....3....4....5....6....7....8....9....10

7.5 *
6.9

ATTENTION TO DETAIL: The ability to pay attention to the specific elements, facets or parts of a situation or work assignment.

0....1....2....3....4....5....6....7....8....9....10

8.0 *
7.5

CONSISTENCY AND RELIABILITY: The capacity to regularly and dependably engage in and complete tasks or processes.

0....1....2....3....4....5....6....7....8....9....10

7.3 *
7.2

PROBLEM SOLVING: The ability to identify key components of the problem, possible solutions and the action plan to obtain the desired result.

0....1....2....3....4....5....6....7....8....9....10

7.5 *
7.5

PROJECT AND GOAL FOCUS: The capacity to concentrate one's full attention on the project or goal at hand, regardless of distractions or difficulties.

0....1....2....3....4....5....6....7....8....9....10

7.4 *
7.3

RESULTS ORIENTATION: The capacity to clearly and objectively understand and implement all variables necessary to obtain defined or desired results.

0....1....2....3....4....5....6....7....8....9....10

7.3 *
6.8

* 68% of the population falls within the shaded area.

Using DISC Behavioral Profiles Before Interviewing Candidates

---

As you can see from these graphical representations, Elizabeth consistently scored highly in almost every area of the PTSI. Based upon the information reflected in this Personal Talent Skills Inventory, along with an evaluation of Elizabeth's DISC behavioral profile, it's immediately apparent that she would make a good candidate for a position on our technical team.

Because we realize the tremendous value the DISC behavioral profile and Personal Talent Skills Inventory offer to any employer, we have created a DISC profile service for our partners which not only allows them to run online DISC profiles for their own staffing requirements, but also affords them the opportunity to re-sell this service to their clients, and earn additional revenue for providing this valuable online service. For more information, and to order a complimentary DISC profile of your own, visit the following link on our website: www.mspu.us/disc.htm.

The Interview Process for Hiring Technical Staff

Now that we've reviewed the DISC behavioral profile and Personal Talent Skills Inventory results of our top candidates, we can decide which of these merit an in-person interview. Note that we have minimized much of the effort we used to expend when hiring staff in the old days. Those were the days when candidates would show up to our offices after sending in a resume that looked promising, and we'd take lots and lots of time out of our busy schedules to interview them. And guess what? Many of the interviews for technical positions went really well – making it difficult for us to choose the right candidate.

Always remember to keep in mind the candidate's current employment situation during the interview and hiring process, and ask pointed questions regarding their prior and current employment history. A great technical candidate should not currently be out of work, unless there is a very compelling reason for it. It's simple logic to assume that successful, aggressive and motivated technical resources worth their salt should currently be employed. And if they are successful, they should look and act the part. A good candidate realizes the value of first impressions and follow-up. If they're not dressed to impress, and speak confidently and articulately during interviews, that's strike one. If they don't initiate good follow-up after interviews, that's strike two. If they are not responsive to your attempts at contact after interviews, that's strike three.

Successful technical candidates will have a firm knowledge of their history at previous employers, and be able to communicate their skill set, certifications and technical experience, in addition to their salaries and bonus plans for the past 3 years. We're also going to ask them specific questions about their daily duties, roles and responsibilities, and how much of their compensation was based upon meeting quotas for utilization, billing, client satisfaction and adhering to SLAs, and how often they failed to achieve them. If they stutter or stammer, or begin tap-dancing during this line of questioning, that's a red flag. And as with any potential hire, spotty or short tenure at previous employers is always a matter for concern. Read between the lines of the candidate's resume, and don't be afraid to ask the tough questions – be direct and look for the same in return. If you're not good at confrontation, for Pete's sake, please have someone else perform these initial interviews for you. The ultimate effectiveness of your service delivery begins with the decisions you make during the hiring process.

Let's take a look at areas to evaluate when interviewing a technical staff candidate (depending upon their experience and areas of expertise, an experienced technical person will qualify themselves by answering the following questions successfully):

- Ask the candidate to verbalize their basic problem management and resolution strategy
- Is the candidate experienced and trained in PSAs, trouble-ticketing systems and RMM solutions? If so, ask them to describe which ones and their experience with them.
- How does the candidate keep up with new technology?
- What are the candidate's certifications?
- What are the candidate's existing utilization numbers at their current/recent position?
- How many service requests does the candidate close per day/week/month at their current/recent position?
- What is the candidate's current/recent job title and function?
- Does the candidate have experience providing proactive, reactive support, or both?
- What percentage of time does the candidate provide remote support at their current/recent position?
- What percentage of time does the candidate provide onsite support at their current/recent position?
- Does the candidate have experience with producing service reports?

- Ask the candidate to describe successful methods they've used to calm an irate user or client with specific examples
- Ask the candidate to provide a history of the hardware they have worked with and to rank their expertise in same
- Ask the candidate to provide a history of the software they have worked with and to rank their expertise in same
- Ask the candidate to provide a history of the solutions they have worked with and to rank their expertise in same
- Ask the candidate to provide a history of the vendors they have worked with and to describe their relationship
- What metrics is the candidate's measured by in their current/recent position and how often do they exceed them?
- What support tier does the candidate currently participate in at their current/recent position?
- How many other technical resources comprise the candidate's business unit at their current/recent position?
- What percentage of time does the candidate spend mentoring other technical resources at their current/recent position?
- What percentage of time does the candidate spend troubleshooting an issue before deciding to escalate it?

- Has the candidate ever managed a team of resources? If so, ask them to describe these situations, their role and responsibilities and success at achieving their objective.
- Verbalize several support scenarios specific to the position the candidate is interviewing for, and ask them how they would approach and resolve them

For an exhaustive list of technical questions to ask the candidate, browse to the following links at Daniel Petri's excellent IT Knowledgebase:

- **Networking:**
  http://www.petri.co.il/mcse_system_administrator_ne tworking_interview_questions.htm
- **Active Directory:**
  http://www.petri.co.il/mcse_system_administrator_ac tive_directory_interview_questions.htm
- **Microsoft Exchange:**
  http://www.petri.co.il/mcse-system-administrator-exchange-interview-questions.htm
- **PC Support:**
  http://www.petri.co.il/mcse-system-administrator-pc-technician-interview-questions.htm

The interview questions contained at the links above on the Petri Knowledgebase are comprehensive – take a look at these when developing your interview and testing process for new technical hires and don't reinvent the wheel.

Based upon review of the Personal Talent Skills Inventory and candidate's performance during the initial interview, determine whether the candidate can qualify to join your technical staff, once they understand your particular processes and procedures, tools and technology.

These are the technical-specific areas we will cover during the initial live interview with all candidates, as well as the technical-specific activities they will be asked to perform during the interview (such as taking a written technical test or troubleshooting a test pc, server or network "sabotaged" for this purpose). The best technical candidates will rise to the top of the list naturally. But let me throw out a cautionary note here – we don't want to make the mistake of hiring the best candidate of the bunch just because they are the best candidate of the bunch. We've got to hire the best candidate for our organization. This means we must be prepared to interview many candidates before making the commitment to hire and train one.

Some general questions we would also like to have answered include:

- What do you know about our company?
    - What we are gauging here is their preparation for the interview – a good candidate would have researched our website, at the very least
- Tell me a little bit about yourself and your previous employment history
    - What we are looking for is a brief description of their work history & skills, a narrative of their personal and professional experiences
- What are some of your strengths?
    - This question should not be difficult for the candidate to answer
- What are some of your weaknesses?
    - A good candidate should not have any trouble naming 3 weaknesses – give them plenty of time to answer
- What do you see yourself doing in 3 years? …. how about in 5 years?
    - Is the candidate a goal-setter?
- Tell me about a time when you made a mistake with a client and what steps you took to resolve the issue
    - Look for awareness of fallibility, and gauge the candidate's problem-resolution technique
- What do you get excited about? …. What upsets you?
- What situations make you lose your temper?
    - These last two questions are more personal in nature, and will be explored in more detail

---

---

   when discussing the candidate's DISC Profile
   with them
- What was one of your greatest successes?
- What are 3 things you do extremely well?
   - A solid candidate will have no trouble
     answering these questions
- What are 3 things that you need to improve on?
   - A good candidate should not have any trouble
     naming all 3 things – give them plenty of time
     to answer
- In a group or team what position do you take on –
  leader, coordinator or support?
   - We're looking for natural leaders here
- Tell us about a team you have worked in
   - What we are looking for is what their role was,
     again to determine if they are a leader,
     facilitator, or socializer
- What are three positive things your last boss would say
  about you?
   - A good candidate should have no problem
     answering this question
- How much guidance and management do you like?
   - We are trying to determine how independent
     the candidate is
- How much do you feel you need?
   - A good candidate will be able to verbalize when
     they need direction
- What type of people do you work best with?

- o This may elicit a canned response, but we may also get a nugget of insight if the person replies, "People who aren't idiots."
- If budgets were of no concern at your current or previous employer, what would be the first thing you would spend money on and why?
  - o The answer to this question gives an insight as to how involved the person was at their previous job. How quickly candidate responds lets us know how much thought they've put into this subject in the past.
- Can you send us an example of something you've written – a quote or proposal?
  - o We need to gauge the candidate's ability to write quotes and proposals, if required
- Is there anything that would interfere with your regular attendance?
  - o A boilerplate question which may reveal any personal conflicts
- What would your perfect job look like?
  - o This is the candidate's opportunity to push the envelope, and test our response – the more descriptive, the better
- Why should we hire you? …. What makes you more qualified than the other applicants?

- o This is the candidate's opportunity to sell us and try to close the position
- What skills do you possess that you think would benefit our company? ....How do you see yourself fitting in?
  - o A follow-up on the previous line of questioning
- Rate yourself on a scale of 1-10 on Word, Excel, PowerPoint, Outlook, Vista...
  - o We're looking for the candidate's proficiency with our basic office applications
- How do you respond to pressure & deadlines?
  - o There isn't a specifically wrong answer here, but we're looking for the candidate's coping mechanism – we might hear: "It stresses me out when...", to which our follow-up would be: "How do you deal with it"?, to which they might answer: "I just get out of the office for a few minutes, and take a walk to clear my head"
- If you could start your career again, what would you do differently?
  - o We're looking for an honest appraisal
- How would you describe your personality?
  - o Easy going, problem solver, director, like talking to people, make friends easily, etc.
- What is your favorite movie of all time? Why?

- Just a question to loosen up the mood, we might find a common interest and chat for a bit
- Describe a time when you made a client/client extremely happy?
    - A positive, reinforcing question
- Do you mind if we call your former employer?
    - A good reason for a negative answer here must be offered
- Why are you considering a career change at this time, or leaving your current position?
- What do you like and dislike about your current position?
    - A couple of basic interview questions meant to provide insight into the candidate's current state of mind and desires
- What about this position do you find the most appealing? .... Least appealing?
    - We're looking for something in addition to the compensation
- In your present position, what internal problems have you identified and taken action to fix?
    - We're gauging how deeply the candidate cares to involve themselves as a change agent for the benefit of others besides themselves
- What kind of feedback have you received from past clients?

- - Expect positive reviews here
- How have you handled negative feedback from clients, or team members?
  - We're looking for a truthful response here – ask for a specific incident
- Give an example of a time where there was a conflict in a team/group that you were involved in and how it was resolved.
  - What did they do, how did they handle it? What we are looking for is the ability to go straight to the source. Telling the boss right away, without telling the person concerned or ignoring the situation and hoping it will go away are not good signs.
- Do you have any questions for us?
  - A good candidate will always have questions

These are all excellent questions to pose to potential candidates for our technical position. I'm certain you can now see why we don't just interview anyone that can fog a mirror – the interview and hiring process is lengthy, and deservedly so – we need to be absolutely certain to do everything in our power to minimize the possibility of hiring the wrong person. If we're going to spend the considerable time and money to hire and train a new technical person, we want an excellent return on our investment.

The Interview Process for Hiring Technical Staff

So let's say we've found one or two candidates that we feel have the "right stuff", and would be a positive addition to our team. Our next step is to schedule an interview with *another member* of our organization. At MSPU, all job candidates for key roles are interviewed by either I or my business partner. If they are a technical candidate, I perform the first live interview, and if they are a sales and marketing candidate, Gary performs the first live interview. Then we swap roles, so Gary gets to perform the second live interview with all technical candidates, and I do the same for the sales and marketing candidates. This second interview will either validate or solidify the decision to hire a candidate, or not. Like it or not, unless we're a seasoned HR or hiring professional, sometimes it's difficult to be completely objective during the interview and hiring process. This is where having another trusted individual available to compare notes with can be invaluable – especially in situations when there needs to be a "tie-breaker" – two equally qualified candidates that we may find challenging to choose between.

In addition, when I'm the second interviewer, I know that the candidate has already passed muster in order to get to me, so I begin exploring other areas that the first interviewer may not have covered – to answer questions about compatibility (will the candidate be able to fit into our culture), and I try to gauge from a gut feeling (I know, the DISC profile doesn't lie!) and comfort level my impression of how easy it will be to work

---

with and integrate the candidate into our organization. I'll ask questions specifically intended to reveal the more personal side of the candidate, like what their taste in movies or T.V. shows is, what they do for recreation, and ask them about their immediate family, as well as their parents and their backgrounds; to get an idea of their stability and support system, and attempt to uncover any stressors that may affect performance on the job. This is all carried out in a friendly, conversational, "get to know me" manner, where I will share personal information with the candidate myself, a la Hannibal Lecter in Silence of the Lambs "...*quid pro quo, Clarisse*...."

If the candidate stands a good chance of joining the team, it's important to begin building a relationship early on. If we really want to win over a candidate, we need to show them the human side of our organization, as well as the career opportunity. Assuming the second interview goes well, we now have a green light to formalize an offer to the successful candidate. During the first interview, items such as compensation and duties and responsibilities would naturally have been discussed, as well as a projected start date of employment, should the candidate be awarded the position.

It's now time to formalize our offer to the successful candidate by means of an offer letter.

The Offer Letter

The offer letter will detail our intent to hire the candidate, what their roles and responsibilities will be, as well as their compensation, bonus and benefits plan. As with any and all forms used in your business practice, please consult with your legal advisor before relying on them.

Let's take a look at a standard offer letter:

Offer of Employment and Employment Contract

Monday, September 1st, 2008

(Employee's Name)

(Employee's Address)

Dear (Employee Name);

We are pleased to offer you a position with MSP University ("Company"). Your start date, manager, compensation, benefits, and other terms of employment will be as set forth below and on EXHIBIT A.

TERMS OF EMPLOYMENT

---

1. **Position and Duties.** Company shall employ you, and you agree to competently and professionally perform such duties as are customarily the responsibility of the position as set forth in the job description attached as EXHIBIT A and as reasonably assigned to you from time to time by your Manager as set forth in EXHIBIT A.

2. **Outside Business Activities.** During your employment with Company, you shall devote competent energies, interests, and abilities to the performance of your duties under this Agreement. During the term of this Agreement, you shall not, without Company's prior written consent, render any services to others for compensation or engage or participate, actively or passively, in any other business activities that would interfere with the performance of your duties hereunder or compete with Company's business.

3. **Employment Classification.** You shall be a Full-Time Employee and shall not be entitled to benefits except as specifically outlined herein.

4. **Compensation/Benefits**.

> 4.1 **Wage.** Company shall pay you the wage as set forth in the job description attached as EXHIBIT A.

> 4.2 **Reimbursement of Expenses**. You shall be reimbursed for all reasonable and necessary expenses

paid or incurred by you in the performance of your duties. You shall provide Company with original receipts for such expenses.

4.3 **Withholdings**. All compensation paid to you under this Agreement, including payment of salary and taxable benefits shall be subject to such withholdings as may be required by law or Company's general practices.

4.4 **Benefits.** You will also receive Company's standard employee benefits package (including health insurance), and will be subject to Company's vacation policy as such package and policy are in effect from time to time.

5. **At-Will Employment.** Either party may terminate this Agreement by written notice at any time for any reason or for no reason. This Agreement is intended to be and shall be deemed to be an at-will employment Agreement and does not constitute a guarantee of continuing employment for any term.

6. **Nondisclosure Agreement.** You agree to sign Company's standard Employee Nondisclosure Agreement, Non-Compete and Proprietary Rights Assignment as a condition of your employment. We wish to impress upon you that we do not wish you to bring with you any confidential or proprietary

material of any former employer or to violate any other obligation to your former employers.

7. **Authorization to Work.** Because of federal regulations adopted in the Immigration Reform and Control Act of 1986, you will need to present documentation demonstrating that you have authorization to work in the United States.

8. **Further Assurances.** Each party shall perform any and all further acts and execute and deliver any documents that are reasonably necessary to carry out the intent of this Agreement.

9. **Notices.** All notices or other communications required or permitted by this Agreement or by law shall be in writing and shall be deemed duly served and given when delivered personally or by facsimile, air courier, certified mail (return receipt requested), postage and fees prepaid, to the party at the address indicated in the signature block or at such other address as a party may request in writing.

10. **Governing Law.** This Agreement shall be governed and interpreted in accordance with the laws of the State of California, as such laws are applied to agreements between residents of California to be performed entirely within the State of California.

---

11. **Entire Agreement.** This Agreement sets forth the entire Agreement between the parties pertaining to the subject matter hereof and supersedes all prior written agreements and all prior or contemporaneous oral Agreements and understandings, expressed or implied.

12. **Written Modification and Waiver.** No modification to this Agreement, nor any waiver of any rights, shall be effective unless assented to in writing by the party to be charged, and the waiver of any breach or default shall not constitute a waiver of any other right or any subsequent breach or default.

13. **Assignment.** This Agreement is personal in nature, and neither of the parties shall, without the consent of the other, assign or transfer this Agreement or any rights or obligations under this Agreement, except that Company may assign or transfer this Agreement to a successor of Company's business, in the event of the transfer or sale of all or substantially all of the assets of Company's business, or to a subsidiary, provided that in the case of any assignment or transfer under the terms of this Section, this Agreement shall be binding on and inure to the benefit of the successor of Company's business, and the successor of Company's business shall discharge and perform all of the obligations of Company under this Agreement.

14. **Severability.** If any of the provisions of this Agreement are determined to be invalid, illegal, or unenforceable, such

---

provisions shall be modified to the minimum extent necessary to make such provisions enforceable, and the remaining provisions shall continue in full force and effect to the extent the economic benefits conferred upon the parties by this Agreement remain substantially unimpaired.

15. **Arbitration of Disputes.** Any controversy or claim arising out of or relating to this contract, or the breach thereof, shall be settled by arbitration administered by the American Arbitration Association under its National Rules for the Resolution of Employment Disputes, and judgment upon the award rendered by the arbitrator(s) may be entered by any court having jurisdiction thereof.

We look forward to your arrival and what we hope will be the start of a mutually satisfying work relationship.

Sincerely,

MSP University

By: _____
    MSPU Authorized Representative

Acknowledged, Accepted, and Agreed

Date: _____

By: _____
      Employee

Once the employee signs the Offer Letter, they will have formally agreed to the terms and conditions of our employment as described. An EXHIBIT A would follow this agreement, stipulating the employee's job description, duties and compensation. Let's review an example EXHIBIT A:

Exhibit "A"

Job Description – Service Desk Analyst

Start Date Is Monday, January 4, 2010

This position will require, but not be limited to the following Essential Responsibilities:

- Provide remote and onsite desktop, laptop, server and network problem management and resolution services to clients and end users via Company's communications and remote and onsite support solutions, processes and procedures
- Identify, document, prioritize, troubleshoot and escalate service requests per Company's problem management and resolution processes and SLAs
- Perform proactive maintenance of client and end user hardware, software and services per Company's established processes and best practices
- Maintain and pursue I.T. training competencies and certifications per Company's established training schedule and requirements
- Maintain Company standards for client satisfaction, utilization and compliance policies
- Utilize Company's PSA and RMM solutions per Company's established processes to deliver maintenance and problem management and resolution services to clients and end users
- Interface with clients, end users and vendor support resources as needed to deliver services within established SLAs
- Maintain communication with all affected parties during problem management and resolution per Company's established processes and procedures

---

Base Salary for this position will be ($) per year.

Eligibility to participate in quarterly bonuses will be determined by meeting established Company utilization, process and policy compliance, attainment of training and competencies/certifications, adherence to SLAs and customer service performance metrics:

Utilization requirement score: (%)

Process and policy compliance score: (%)

Attainment of competencies: (%)

Adherence to SLAs score: (%)

Customer service score: (%)

Of course, your particular business model, products, services job requirements and compensation schedules will dictate how you structure EXHIBIT A.

The Employment Agreement

As part of the HR and hiring process, we are going to require our new technical person to sign an employment agreement. The employment agreement will detail the technical person's job title and duties and responsibilities, and will contain non-disclosure and non-compete language in order to protect ourselves from the potential for one of our competitors to hire our technical person away at some later date, and leverage our business plans, processes or other intellectual property against us. Depending upon your local or state laws, NDA and non-compete language and/or agreements will need to be tailored specifically to protect your rights in a court of law. As with any and all forms used in your business practice, please consult with your legal advisor before relying on them.

Let's take a look at a standard Employment Agreement:

EMPLOYMENT AGREEMENT

This Employment Agreement (this "Agreement") is made effective by and between MSP University ("MSPU"), of 7077 Orangewood Avenue, Suite 104, Garden Grove, California, 92841 and (employee's name) ("Employee"), of (employee's address).

A. MSPU is engaged in the business of Providing Information Technology Services. Employee will primarily perform the job duties at the following location: 7077 Orangewood Avenue, Suite 104, Garden Grove, California.

B. MSPU desires to have the services of Employee.

C. Employee is willing to be employed by MSPU.

Therefore, the parties agree as follows:

1. EMPLOYMENT. MSPU shall employ Employee as a (job title). Employee shall provide to MSPU the following services: duties as needed. Employee accepts and agrees to such employment, and agrees to be subject to the general supervision, advice and direction of MSPU and MSPU's supervisory personnel. Employee shall also perform (i) such other duties as are customarily performed by an employee in a similar position, and (ii) such other and unrelated services and duties as may be assigned to Employee from time to time by MSPU.

2. BEST EFFORTS OF EMPLOYEE. Employee agrees to perform faithfully, industriously, and to the best of Employee's ability, experience, and talents, all of the duties that may be required by the express and implicit terms of this Agreement, to the reasonable satisfaction of MSPU. Such duties shall be

provided at such place(s) as the needs, business, or opportunities of MSPU may require from time to time.

3. EXPENSE REIMBURSEMENT. MSPU will reimburse Employee for "out-of-pocket" expenses incurred by Employee in accordance with MSPU policies in effect from time to time.

4. RECOMMENDATIONS FOR IMPROVING OPERATIONS. Employee shall provide MSPU with all information, suggestions, and recommendations regarding MSPU's business, of which Employee has knowledge, which will be of benefit to MSPU.

5. CONFIDENTIALITY. Employee recognizes that MSPU has and will have information regarding the following:

- inventions

- products

- product design

- processes

- technical matters

- trade secrets

- copyrights

- client lists

The Employment Agreement

- prices

- costs

- discounts

- business affairs

- future plans

- marketing plans and methods

- communications

- meetings

- conversations

- training

- emails

- faxes

- documents

- wage and compensation information

- disciplinary actions

- policies

---

and other vital information items (collectively, "Information") which are valuable, special and unique assets of MSPU. Employee agrees that Employee will not at any time or in any manner, either directly or indirectly, divulge, disclose, or communicate any Information to any third party without the prior written consent of MSPU. Employee will protect the Information and treat it as strictly confidential. A violation by Employee of this paragraph shall be a material violation of this Agreement and will justify legal and/or equitable relief.

6. UNAUTHORIZED DISCLOSURE OF INFORMATION. If it appears that Employee has disclosed (or has threatened to disclose) Information in violation of this Agreement, MSPU shall be entitled to an injunction to restrain Employee from disclosing, in whole or in part, such Information, or from providing any services to any party to whom such Information has been disclosed or may be disclosed. MSPU shall not be prohibited by this provision from pursuing other remedies, including a claim for losses and damages.

7. CONFIDENTIALITY AFTER TERMINATION OF EMPLOYMENT. The confidentiality provisions of this Agreement shall remain in full force and effect for a 1 year period after the termination of Employee's employment.

8. NON-COMPETE AGREEMENT. Employee recognizes that the various items of Information are special and unique assets

of the Company and need to be protected from improper disclosure. In consideration of the disclosure of the Information to Employee, Employee agrees and covenants that for a period of 1 year following the termination of this Agreement, whether such termination is voluntary or involuntary, Employee will not compete directly or indirectly with MSPU. The term "not compete" shall mean that the Employee shall not, on Employee's behalf or on behalf of any other party, solicit or seek the business of any client or account of the Company existing during the term of employment and wherein said solicitation involves a product and/or service substantially similar to or competitive with any present or future product and/or service of the Company. This covenant shall apply to the geographical area that includes all of the State of California and any other state in which the Company has clients. Directly or indirectly engaging in any competitive business includes, but is not limited to: (i) engaging in a business as owner, partner, or agent, (ii) becoming an employee of any third party that is engaged in such business, (iii) becoming interested directly or indirectly in any such business, or (iv) soliciting any client of MSPU for the benefit of a third party that is engaged in such business. Employee agrees that this non-compete provision will not adversely affect Employee's livelihood.

9. EMPLOYEE'S INABILITY TO CONTRACT FOR EMPLOYER.
Employee shall not have the right to make any contracts or

---

commitments for or on behalf of MSPU without first obtaining the express written consent of MSPU.

10. BENEFITS. Employee shall be entitled to employment benefits, including holidays, sick leave, and vacation as provided by MSPU's policies in effect from time to time.

11. TERM/TERMINATION. Employee's employment under this Agreement shall be for an unspecified term on an "at will" basis. This Agreement may be terminated by MSPU at will and by Employee upon 2 Week's written notice. If Employee is in violation of any part of this Agreement, MSPU may terminate employment without notice and with compensation to Employee only to the date of such termination. The compensation paid under this Agreement shall be Employee's exclusive remedy.

12. COMPLIANCE WITH EMPLOYER'S RULES. Employee agrees to comply with all of the rules and regulations of MSPU.

13. RETURN OF PROPERTY. Upon termination of this Agreement, Employee shall deliver to MSPU all property which is MSPU's property or related to MSPU's business (including keys, records, notes, data, memoranda, models, and equipment) that is in Employee's possession or under Employee's control. Such obligation shall be governed by any separate confidentiality or proprietary rights agreement signed by Employee.

---

14. NOTICES. All notices required or permitted under this Agreement shall be in writing and shall be deemed delivered when delivered in person or on the third day after being deposited in the United States mail, postage paid, addressed as follows:

Employer:

MSPU

(MSPU Representative)

(MSPU Representative's title)

7077 Orangewood Avenue, Suite 104

Garden Grove, California 92841

Employee:

(Employee Name)

(Employee Street Address)

(Employee City, State ZIP)

Such addresses may be changed from time to time by either party by providing written notice in the manner set forth above.

15. ENTIRE AGREEMENT. This Agreement contains the entire agreement of the parties and there are no other promises or conditions in any other agreement whether oral or written. This Agreement supersedes any prior written or oral agreements between the parties.

16. AMENDMENT. This Agreement may be modified or amended, if the amendment is made in writing and is signed by both parties.

17. SEVERABILITY. If any provisions of this Agreement shall be held to be invalid or unenforceable for any reason, the remaining provisions shall continue to be valid and enforceable. If a court finds that any provision of this Agreement is invalid or unenforceable, but that by limiting such provision it would become valid or enforceable, then such provision shall be deemed to be written, construed, and enforced as so limited.

18. WAIVER OF CONTRACTUAL RIGHT. The failure of either party to enforce any provision of this Agreement shall not be construed as a waiver or limitation of that party's right to subsequently enforce and compel strict compliance with every provision of this Agreement.

19. APPLICABLE LAW. This Agreement shall be governed by the laws of the State of California.

EMPLOYER:

MSP University

By: _____Date: _____

(Authorized MSPU representative name/title)

AGREED TO AND ACCEPTED.

EMPLOYEE:

By: _____Date: _____

The Equipment Loan Agreement

From time to time, and based upon the technical staff's needs, it may become necessary to supply them with company-owned equipment in order to provide them the ability to fulfill their duties and responsibilities. Examples of equipment that can be furnished to employees may include:

- Vehicles
- PCs
- Laptops
- Wireless PC cards
- Cell phones/Smart phones/PDAs
- Pagers
- Security tokens
- Key cards/credentials
- Test equipment
- Inventory

This equipment obviously has value to the company, so it is a good idea to have a solid equipment loan agreement in place documenting it and its value, and holding the employee responsible for keeping it in good condition. The equipment loan agreement also makes it easier to reclaim equipment when an employee leaves the organization, as they agree to forfeit the cost to replace the equipment from their pay

---

---

should they fail to return it according to the terms of their employment agreement. Let's take a look at a standard equipment loan agreement:

Equipment Loan

Statement of Understanding

I am taking possession of the following equipment belonging to MSP University (Company):

_____

Description

_____

Model Number, Serial Number

which has a replacement cost of $

_____

I will take reasonable and necessary steps to safeguard this equipment from damage and theft.

The Best NOC and Service Desk Operations BOOK EVER!

The Equipment Loan Agreement

If this equipment is damaged or stolen, I will report the relevant facts as soon as possible to my supervisor. I further understand that I have an obligation to pursue recovery for Company from such a loss through my relevant insurance coverage, whether automobile, homeowner's or tenant's.

I understand that I must return this equipment as instructed to Company premises within twenty-four hours of being asked to do so by my supervisor or Company administration.

I understand that I must immediately return this equipment as instructed to Company premises in the event that my employment ends, whether by voluntary quit or involuntary termination.

I agree and hereby give permission to Company to deduct from my pay any amount I owe to Company (up to the replacement cost noted above) due to my failure to return this equipment in working condition to Company as documented in my Employment Agreement.

_____

Employee Signature, printed name and date

_____

Date EQUIPMENT RETURNED:

_____

Received By

Compensation Plans

Throughout the years we've had the opportunity to work with our partners, one of the topics that seem to be the most challenging for them is creating an equitable compensation plan for technical staff. Now, as IT service providers, our perception of an equitable compensation plan and our technical staff's perception of an equitable compensation plan may not always match. A generally accepted industry statistic regarding compensation is that a technician should generate two and a half times their W-2 compensation in billable labor time. This means that a technical person earning $60,000 a year on their W-2 should be generating $150,000 in billable labor time per year.

Billable time based on W-2 earnings

W-2 Earnings	Billable Labor
$30,000	$75,000
$40,000	$100,000
$50,000	$125,000
$60,000	$150,000
$70,000	$175,000
$80,000	$200,000
$90,000	$225,000
$100,000	$250,000

Salary.com reports the following U.S. national averages for total compensation (base salaries, bonuses and benefits) for the following technical positions as of January, 2010 on their website at http://swz.salary.com/salarywizard/layoutscripts/swzl_newsearch.asp:

Help Desk Support Jr.-Sr. (Service Desk Staff)

Benefit	Median Amount		% Of Total	
Base Salary	$44,900	$52,608	68.5% -	69.4%
Bonuses	$906	$1,135	1.4% -	1.5%
Social Security	$3,504	$4,111	5.3% -	5.4%
401k/403b	$1,741	$2,042	2.7% -	2.7%
Disability	$458	$537	0.7% -	0.7%
Healthcare	$6,103	$6,103	9.3% -	8.0%
Pension	$2,290	$2,687	3.5% -	3.5%
Time Off	$5,638	$6,615	8.6% -	8.7%
Total	$65,540	$75,839	100%	

Source: salary.com

Please note that the median Service Desk staff's bonuses in the US as reported in January 2010 by salary.com amount to about 1.5% of their total take-home compensation. In our experience, this is extremely low, as we would bonus our

---

Service Desk staff upwards of 10% of their total salary for achieving goals set for:

- Utilization requirements
- Process and policy compliance
- Attainment of competencies
- Adherence to SLAs
- Customer service

We would base customer service scores upon survey responses. In addition, bonuses could be attained individually and by the entire group on a monthly, quarterly and yearly basis. This was designed so that if an individual resource achieved their minimum goals in each area for the month, they would be eligible to receive a bonus. If they achieved the bonus each month for the entire quarter, they would be eligible to receive a quarterly bonus as well. If the entire team achieved their bonuses each month in a quarter, they would be eligible to receive a quarterly team bonus, and if they were able to achieve a quarterly team bonus through 4 consecutive quarters, they would be eligible to receive a yearly bonus. All of these bonuses would be in addition to previously-received bonuses, so the individual Service Desk staff could potentially be eligible to receive the following bonuses:

- Monthly individual bonus
- Quarterly individual bonus

- Quarterly team bonus
- Yearly team bonus

Service Dispatcher Jr.-Sr.

Benefit	Median Amount		% Of Total	
Base Salary	$34,910	$42,063	67.1% -	68.2%
Bonuses	$475	$764	0.9% -	1.2%
Social Security	$2,707	$3,276	5.2% -	5.3%
401k/403b	$1,345	$1,627	2.6% -	2.6%
Disability	$354	$428	0.7% -	0.7%
Healthcare	$6,103	$6,103	11.7% -	9.9%
Pension	$1,769	$2,141	3.4% -	3.5%
Time Off	$4,355	$5,271	8.4% -	8.5%
Total	$52,017	$61,674	100%	

Source: salary.com

Note that the median service dispatcher's bonuses in the US as reported in January 2010 by salary.com amount to about 1.2% of their total take-home compensation. This is low in our experience, as we bonused our dispatcher a small amount based upon meeting SLAs, along with allowing participation in team bonuses, but their bonus did not quite rival the Service Desk staff's.

Compensation Plans

Service Desk Manager

Benefit	Median Amount	% Of Total
Base Salary	$84,146	67.7%
Bonuses	$6,923	5.6%
Social Security	$6,967	5.6%
401k/403b	$3,461	2.8%
Disability	$911	0.7%
Healthcare	$6,103	4.9%
Pension	$4,553	3.7%
Time Off	$11,208	9.0%
Total	$124,272	100%

Source: salary.com

Note that the median Service Desk manager's bonuses in the US as reported in January 2010 by salary.com average 5.6% of their total take-home compensation. This matches our experience.

NOC Manager

Benefit	Median Amount	% Of Total
Base Salary	$95,508	70.5%
Bonuses	$4,250	3.1%
Social Security	$7,708	5.6%
401k/403b	$3,849	2.8%
Disability	$1,008	0.7%
Healthcare	$6,103	4.5%
Pension	$5,038	3.7%
Time Off	$12,401	9.1%
Total	$136,844	100%

Source: salary.com

Note that the median NOC manager's bonuses in the US as reported in January 2010 by salary.com average about 3.1% of their total take-home compensation. This matches our experience.

A compensation plan for a new technical person will normally be structured as base salary plus bonuses. A base salary is a guaranteed amount of compensation the technical person will receive each month, and if they meet specific goals set by

---

---

their supervisor during the month, quarter and year, additional bonuses can be realized.

In a base plus bonus compensation plan, we generally see small bonus percentages structured in to support the guaranteed base salary, and engineered in such a manner as to reward the technical staff on activity that helps the organization increase efficiencies and client satisfaction, among other factors – all of which in one form or another drive additional profits to the bottom line. This is where the bonuses are paid out from – the additional revenues that the technical staff helps to generate.

Now I hope I've done a decent job of presenting different ways of looking at technical compensation and bonus plans for you. Please do not take any of the figures in this chapter as gospel – but rather visit salary.com to drill deep and utilize their filtering capabilities and input your zip code, state or metro area to discover what the median compensation is being reported for the technical roles required for your service delivery model and mode. I've used information gathered from partners, and the rest from our own experience to help you get started.

If you'd like a much more granular compensation report, browse to www.mspu.us/en/tools and pick up the Service Leadership Index™ 2009 Solution Provider Compensation

---

Report™. This 100-page report covers more than 40 positions in solution provider practices and is the only solution-provider-specific salary survey available.

Let me caution you against thinking that by reading this chapter you will be able to save yourself some homework and come away with a ready-made compensation plan that you can simply slap your company's name on, implement and be successful with.

You've got to do your own legwork and investigation into what your true margins and profitability are for each of your services, products and solutions. From there, you've got to dig down deep into your gut and come up with a realistic expectation of how much increased profitability each of your technical resources can achieve, and of this number, what you are comfortable with incenting your staff to qualify for.

Training Technical Staff

The function of training technical staff in an IT services organization, NOC or Service Desk is obviously much different than training staff in other businesses or business units. In addition to training technical staff in NOC and Service Desk overall day-to-day operations and functions, there need to be opportunities for technical staff to receive the role-specific training required to make them effective, efficient and successful, in order to receive the maximum return on their hiring investment.

Let's identify the common training that will be delivered to all staff, regardless of their job description, before going into role-specific technical training topics:

- Company Overview Training
  - Vision, mission, values, philosophy, goals
- HR Process Training
  - Overview of compensation, benefits, conduct, sick day and vacation policy, Employee handbook, acceptable use policy
- Administrative Setup and Training
  - User and email account creation, telco account, extension and voicemail creation,
  - Use of company equipment (cell phone, PC, laptop, etc.)

- Use of company software, Instant Messaging, remote access and remote email
- Formal introduction to management and staff
  - Tour of facility
  - Introduction to all management and staff

The above points cover in broad strokes some of the tasks associated with any new employee's basic training and indoctrination to an organization – of course, the outsourced service provider's or internal service manager's policies and procedures may differ from those illustrated.

So what role-specific training is needed to deliver to insure a technical person's success? Let's highlight some of the obvious areas for their managers to address:

- Internal tools and technology training
  - Make certain all technical staff is trained on internal tools
    - PSA solution
    - RMM solution
    - Remote control solution
    - Quoting solution
    - Technical drawing solution
    - Project planning/management solution
    - Specialty solutions

- All others

- Processes and procedures
  - Make certain all technical staff is trained on all processes and procedures
    - Employee handbook
    - Incident management, escalation and resolution
    - Remote monitoring and management
    - Remote control
    - Patching and updating
    - Documentation
    - Customer service
    - Reporting
    - All others
- Product and Service Training
  - Make certain all technical staff is trained on all of products and services delivered
- Roles and responsibilities
  - Make certain all technical staff is trained on their own, as well as other team members' roles, responsibilities and expectations
- Clients
  - Make certain all technical staff is trained on the organization's clients and their individual needs, requirements and SLAs

- Fulfillment partners
  - Make certain all technical staff is trained on the organization's fulfillment partners, their services and their engagement process
- Vendors
  - Make certain all technical staff is trained on the organization's vendors, their services and their engagement process
- Goals and bonuses
  - Make certain all technical staff is trained on their individual and team goals and bonus programs
- Competency and certification achievement
  - Make certain all technical staff is trained on the organization's requirements for their attainment of additional competencies and certifications

Role-Specific Training

NOC staff
In this context, the NOC staff participates in the outsourced service provider's or internal service manager's incident management and resolution process, and can be assigned to deliver proactive remote patching, updating and monitoring services for devices, operating systems, applications software and services in client environments. Whereas the Service Desk

staff works primarily with end user issues, the NOC staff's main focus is on managing and delivering scheduled maintenance activities to critical devices and responding to alerts generated by the provider's Remote Monitoring and Management solution.

The NOC staff identifies, prioritizes and documents all service activity and will execute the outsourced service provider's or internal service manager's incident management and resolution processes as well as utilize the provider's chosen software and hardware management and remediation tools, processes and procedures during remote service delivery.

In addition to the general training requirements for all technical staff previously mentioned, at a minimum, all NOC staff will need specific training in these areas:

- Problem management and resolution
  - Incident Management
  - Problem Management
  - Configuration Management
  - Change Management
  - Risk Management
  - Release Management
  - Service Level Management
  - Availability Management
  - Capacity Management
  - Service Continuity Management
  - Security Management

- o Communication Management
- Remote Monitoring and Management
  - o Installing agents
  - o Configuring thresholds
  - o Configuring alerts
  - o Developing scripts
  - o Incident Management
  - o Problem Management
  - o Configuration Management
  - o Change Management
  - o Risk Management
  - o Release Management
  - o Service level management
  - o Availability Management
  - o Capacity Management
  - o Service Continuity Management
  - o Security Management
  - o Communications Management
- Day to day service delivery
  - o Receiving all incident notifications and service requests
  - o Recording all incidents and service requests
  - o Classifying all incidents and service requests
  - o Prioritizing all incidents and service requests
  - o Troubleshooting all incidents and service requests
  - o Escalating all incidents and service requests as necessary to maintain SLA

- o Maintaining consistent communication with all parties affected by the incident or service request
  - o Performing all scheduled maintenance activities
  - o Reporting on all activities
- Customer service
  - o Customer management
  - o Setting and adjusting expectations
  - o Phone etiquette
  - o Utilizing the "hold" or "mute" button effectively
  - o Follow-up and follow-through

Service Desk staff

In this context, the Service Desk staff participates in the outsourced service provider's or internal service manager's incident management and resolution process, and can be assigned to deliver remote technical support services to end users. The Service Desk staff identifies, prioritizes and documents all service requests, and initiates incident management and resolution activity.

Service desk staff will execute the outsourced service provider's or internal service manager's incident management and resolution processes as well as utilize the provider's chosen software and hardware management and remediation tools, processes and procedures during remote technical service delivery.

In addition to the general training requirements for all technical staff previously mentioned, at a minimum, all Service Desk staff will need specific training in these areas:

- Problem management and resolution
  - Incident Management
  - Problem Management
  - Configuration Management
  - Change Management
  - Risk Management
  - Release Management
  - Service Level Management
  - Availability Management
  - Capacity Management
  - IT Service Continuity Management
  - Security Management
  - Communication Management
- Day to day service delivery
  - Receiving all incident notifications and service requests
  - Recording all incidents and service requests
  - Classifying all incidents and service requests
  - Prioritizing all incidents and service requests
  - Troubleshooting all incidents and service requests
  - Escalating all incidents and service requests as necessary to maintain SLA
  - Maintaining consistent communication with all parties affected by the incident or service request

- o Performing all scheduled maintenance activities
- o Reporting on all activities
- Customer service
  - o Customer management
  - o Setting and adjusting expectations
  - o Phone etiquette
  - o Utilizing the "hold" or "mute" button effectively
  - o Follow-up and follow-through

Service Dispatchers

In this context, the service dispatcher participates in the outsourced service provider's or internal service manager's incident management and resolution process, and assigns resources to and schedules all services. The service dispatcher may also be included in the provider's escalation process and be alerted by their PSA solution should service requests become in danger of falling out of SLA.

Service dispatchers will utilize the provider's chosen software management tools, processes and procedures to manage dispatch functions during technical service delivery.

In addition to the general training requirements for all technical staff previously mentioned, at a minimum, all service dispatchers will need specific training in these areas:

- Problem management and resolution
  - o Incident Management

- o Problem Management
- o Configuration Management
- o Change Management
- o Risk Management
- o Release Management
- o Service Level Management
- o Availability Management
- o Capacity Management
- o IT Service Continuity Management
- o Security Management
- o Communication Management
- Day to day service delivery
  - o Managing all incident notifications and service requests
  - o Monitoring all incidents and service requests for proper escalation as necessary to maintain SLA
  - o Managing consistent communication with all parties affected by the incident or service request
  - o Scheduling all maintenance activities
  - o Reporting on all activities
- Customer service
  - o Customer management
  - o Setting and adjusting expectations
  - o Phone etiquette
  - o Utilizing the "hold" or "mute" button effectively
  - o Follow-up and follow-through

NOC Managers

In this context, the NOC manager is ultimately responsible for maintaining the outsourced service provider's or internal service manager's NOC staffing levels, training and certification requirements, incident management and resolution processes and client satisfaction by strict SLA management, among other responsibilities. NOC managers will utilize the provider's chosen software management tools, processes and procedures to manage service delivery.

In addition to the general training requirements for all technical staff previously mentioned, at a minimum, all Service Desk managers will need specific training in these areas:

- Problem management and resolution
  - Incident Management
  - Problem Management
  - Configuration Management
  - Change Management
  - Risk Management
  - Release Management
  - Service Level Management
  - Availability Management
  - Capacity Management
  - Service Continuity Management
  - Security Management
  - Communication Management
- Remote Monitoring and Management
  - Installing agents

- o Configuring thresholds
- o Configuring alerts
- o Developing scripts
- o Incident Management
- o Problem Management
- o Configuration Management
- o Change Management
- o Risk Management
- o Release Management
- o Service level management
- o Availability Management
- o Capacity Management
- o Service Continuity Management
- o Security Management
- o Communications Management
- Day to day service delivery
  - o Receiving all incident notifications and service requests
  - o Recording all incidents and service requests
  - o Classifying all incidents and service requests
  - o Prioritizing all incidents and service requests
  - o Troubleshooting all incidents and service requests
  - o Escalating all incidents and service requests as necessary to maintain SLA
  - o Maintaining consistent communication with all parties affected by the incident or service request
  - o Performing all scheduled maintenance activities
  - o Reporting on all activities

- Customer service
    - Customer management
    - Setting and adjusting expectations
    - Phone etiquette
    - Utilizing the "hold" or "mute" button effectively
    - Follow-up and follow-through

Service Desk Managers

In this context, the Service Desk manager is ultimately responsible for maintaining the outsourced service provider's or internal service manager's Service Desk staffing levels, training and certification requirements, incident management and resolution processes and client satisfaction by strict SLA management, among other responsibilities. Service Desk managers will utilize the provider's chosen software management tools, processes and procedures to manage service delivery.

In addition to the general training requirements for all technical staff previously mentioned, at a minimum, all Service Desk managers will need specific training in these areas:

- Problem management and resolution
    - Incident Management
    - Problem Management
    - Configuration Management
    - Change Management
    - Risk Management

- o Release Management
- o Service Level Management
- o Availability Management
- o Capacity Management
- o IT Service Continuity Management
- o Security Management
- o Communication Management
- Day to day service delivery
    - o Responsible for managing all technical staff
    - o Responsible for managing all service delivery
    - o Responsible for managing all client expectations
    - o Responsible for reporting on all activities
- Customer service
    - o Staff management
    - o Customer management
    - o Setting and adjusting expectations
    - o Follow-up and follow-through

Section 7: NOC and Service Desk Management by the Numbers

In order to reduce costs, improve performance and efficiencies and drive more profit to the bottom line, best in class service providers utilize a means to regularly measure the performance of the NOC and Service Desk. This measurement must focus on capturing *meaningful data* and displaying it in a simple to understand manner. This data will become the Key Performance Indicators by which performance will be measured, goals set against and bonuses and commissions designed and implemented to help realize.

After determining the meaningful data to collect, performance reports can be created to report on this data. These performance reports will be produced and reviewed on a regular basis by the outsourced service provider or internal service manager and their NOC and Service Desk managers.

The first time this KPI data is reported, it must be analyzed to determine a baseline – what is the NOC and Service Desk's performance today? Through this analysis, a true understanding of performance can be realized, which may directly contradict perceived performance up to this point. There are several areas the outsourced service provider or internal service manager and their NOC and Service Desk managers should focus on, but at a minimum should include:

- Financial performance
- NOC performance
- Service Desk performance

Measuring Financial Performance

Measuring financial performance will provide the following information to the outsourced service provider or internal service manager:

- Revenue by product or service sold
- Cost of goods sold by product or service
- Gross margin by product or service sold
- Operating expenses
- Pre-tax net income

Many service providers tend to aggregate all services such as break-fix, time and materials, projects, managed services (including NOC and Service Desk), hosting and license renewals and others into one line item in their accounting system's chart of accounts: service revenue. Setting up the chart of accounts in this manner hampers the ability to understand how well or poorly any individual product or service is financially performing.

Paul Dippell from Service Leadership Inc. (www.service-leadership.com); an advisory firm that specializes in growth, performance and M&A strategies for the IT industry, characterizes this scenario as one of having a relay team of four runners. In this example, each runner represents one deliverable such as break-fix services, project services, managed services, and other services.

Measuring Financial Performance

While the relay team finishes the race with a total time of two minutes and thirty seconds, because the individual split time for each runner is not being measured, it is impossible to determine how fast or slow each runner ran their portion of the race. This prevents the coach from knowing how to improve each individual runner's performance.

The same holds true with outsourced service providers or internal service managers that cannot determine the performance of their individual services in terms of cost, revenue and net profit. The first step in gaining visibility into these areas is to separate the individual revenue streams, their costs and gross margins. Only after this has been done can more meaningful analysis begin.

When evaluating financial performance, special attention should be paid to the differential between the cost of goods sold (COGS) and gross margin (GM) for each product or service sold or delivered; along with their individual contribution to gross revenue, to determine performance and profitability. In addition, a careful review of sales, general & administrative expenses (SG&A), will help identify opportunities to reduce costs in these areas.

Once the outsourced service provider's or internal service manager's financial chart of accounts has been normalized in this fashion, they can develop strategies to continually improve net profits, utilizing regular financial reporting and

---

---

benchmarking to attain this goal by running their organization by the numbers.

Visit MSP University's website at www.mpsu.us/en/tools to download the Service Leadership Index Fundamental Diagnostic Report© to help you diagnose your financial performance effectively and develop prescriptive actions to improve net profits.

Measuring NOC Performance

Measuring NOC performance will provide the outsourced service provider or internal service manager and their NOC manager and staff a clear indicator of performance. Measuring this performance will establish a baseline for improvement, allowing goals for improvement to be set, and bonuses and commissions developed to help incent this improvement.

Key NOC performance indicators that the outsourced service provider or internal service manager will measure may include:

- Total ticket load per day/week/month/quarter/year
- Total ticket load per queue per day/week/month/quarter/year
- Total ticket load per client/location/contract per day/week/month/quarter/year
- Total ticket load per resource per day/week/month/quarter/year
- Average time to resolution per day/week/month/quarter/year
- Average time to resolution per queue per day/week/month/quarter/year

- Average time to resolution per resource per day/week/month/quarter/year
- Average time to resolution per client/location/contract per day/week/month/quarter/year
- Average time to response per day/week/month/quarter/year
- Average time to response per queue per day/week/month/quarter/year
- Average time to response per resource per day/week/month/quarter/year
- Average time to response per client/location/contract per day/week/month/quarter/year
- Total tickets closed per day/week/month/quarter/year
- Total tickets closed per queue per day/week/month/quarter/year
- Total tickets closed per resource per day/week/month/quarter/year
- Total tickets closed per client/location/contract per day/week/month/quarter/year
- Total "Repeat" tickets per day/week/month/quarter/year
- Total "Repeat" tickets per queue per day/week/month/quarter/year
- Total "Repeat" tickets per resource per day/week/month/quarter/year

---

- Total "Repeat" tickets per client/location/contract per day/week/month/quarter/year
- Adherence to SLA % per day/week/month/quarter/year
- Adherence to SLA % per queue per day/week/month/quarter/year
- Adherence to SLA % per resource per day/week/month/quarter/year
- Adherence to SLA % per client/location/contract per day/week/month/quarter/year
- Top Clients with the most open tickets per day/week/month/quarter/year
- Total Cost of Service Delivery per day/week/month/quarter/year
- Total Cost of Service Delivery per queue per day/week/month/quarter/year
- Total Cost of Service Delivery per client/location/contract per day/week/month/quarter/year
- Total Cost of Service Delivery resource per day/week/month/quarter/year
- Utilization per day/week/month/quarter/year
- Utilization per queue per day/week/month/quarter/year
- Utilization per client/location/contract per day/week/month/quarter/year

---

- Utilization per resource per day/week/month/quarter/year
- Realization per day/week/month/quarter/year
- Realization per queue per day/week/month/quarter/year
- Realization per client/location/contract per day/week/month/quarter/year
- Realization per resource per day/week/month/quarter/year
- Profitability per day/week/month/quarter/year
- Profitability per queue day/week/month/quarter/year
- Profitability per client/location/contract per day/week/month/quarter/year
- Profitability per resource per day/week/month/quarter/year
- Client satisfaction per day/week/month/quarter/year
- End user satisfaction per day/week/month/quarter/year
- Resource satisfaction per day/week/month/quarter/year

Measuring Service Desk Performance

Measuring Service Desk performance will provide the outsourced service provider or internal service manager and their Service Desk manager and staff a clear indicator of performance. Measuring this performance will establish a baseline for improvement, allowing goals for improvement to be set, and bonuses and commissions developed to help incent this improvement.

While similar to key NOC performance indicators, with additional metrics included for verbal interaction with clients and end users, key Service Desk performance indicators that the outsourced service provider or internal service manager will measure may include:

- Average speed of call answer per day/week/month/quarter/year
- Average speed of call answer per queue per day/week/month/quarter/year
- Average speed of call answer per resource per day/week/month/quarter/year
- Average speed of call answer per client/location/contract per day/week/month/quarter/year

- Average call wait time per day/week/month/quarter/year
- Average call wait time per queue per day/week/month/quarter/year
- Average call wait time per resource per day/week/month/quarter/year
- Average call wait time per client/location/contract per day/week/month/quarter/year
- Average first call resolution per day/week/month/quarter/year
- Average first call resolution per queue per day/week/month/quarter/year
- Average first call resolution per resource per day/week/month/quarter/year
- Average first call resolution per client/location/contract per day/week/month/quarter/year
- Total ticket load per day/week/month/quarter/year
- Total ticket load per queue per day/week/month/quarter/year
- Total ticket load per client/location/contract per day/week/month/quarter/year
- Total ticket load per resource per day/week/month/quarter/year
- Average time to resolution per day/week/month/quarter/year

- Average time to resolution per queue per day/week/month/quarter/year
- Average time to resolution per resource per day/week/month/quarter/year
- Average time to resolution per client/location/contract per day/week/month/quarter/year
- Average time to response per day/week/month/quarter/year
- Average time to response per queue per day/week/month/quarter/year
- Average time to response per resource per day/week/month/quarter/year
- Average time to response per client/location/contract per day/week/month/quarter/year
- Total tickets closed per day/week/month/quarter/year
- Total tickets closed per queue per day/week/month/quarter/year
- Total tickets closed per resource per day/week/month/quarter/year
- Total tickets closed per client/location/contract per day/week/month/quarter/year
- Total "Repeat" tickets per day/week/month/quarter/year
- Total "Repeat" tickets per queue per day/week/month/quarter/year

- Total "Repeat" tickets per resource per day/week/month/quarter/year
- Total "Repeat" tickets per client/location/contract per day/week/month/quarter/year
- Adherence to SLA % per day/week/month/quarter/year
- Adherence to SLA % per queue per day/week/month/quarter/year
- Adherence to SLA % per resource per day/week/month/quarter/year
- Adherence to SLA % per client/location/contract per day/week/month/quarter/year
- Top Clients with the most open tickets per day/week/month/quarter/year
- Total Cost of Service Delivery per day/week/month/quarter/year
- Total Cost of Service Delivery per queue per day/week/month/quarter/year
- Total Cost of Service Delivery per client/location/contract per day/week/month/quarter/year
- Total Cost of Service Delivery resource per day/week/month/quarter/year
- Utilization per day/week/month/quarter/year
- Utilization per queue per day/week/month/quarter/year

- Utilization per client/location/contract per day/week/month/quarter/year
- Utilization per resource per day/week/month/quarter/year
- Realization per day/week/month/quarter/year
- Realization per queue per day/week/month/quarter/year
- Realization per client/location/contract per day/week/month/quarter/year
- Realization per resource per day/week/month/quarter/year
- Profitability per day/week/month/quarter/year
- Profitability per queue day/week/month/quarter/year
- Profitability per client/location/contract per day/week/month/quarter/year
- Profitability per resource per day/week/month/quarter/year
- Client satisfaction per day/week/month/quarter/year
- End user satisfaction per day/week/month/quarter/year
- Resource satisfaction per day/week/month/quarter/year

The outsourced service provider's or internal service manager's NOC and Service Desk managers should be able to pull the data required to report on these metrics from their

---

Professional Services Automation solution when integrated with their Remote Monitoring and Management tool, their Communications solution and the results of customer satisfaction surveys, in order to identify, evaluate and improve upon these service delivery KPIs.

Section 8: Outsourcing NOC and Service Desk Components

With the advent of affordable, 3rd-party back office NOC and Service Desk organizations, the outsourced service provider or internal service manager has the opportunity to scale their services to a much broader range of clients, and prolong the necessity to hire, train and manage internal full-time staff. This allows a consistent support experience for clients and end users and in many cases increases the provider's profitability due to the low cost of these services. In addition, these organizations can private-label their services, and represent the outsourced service provider's or internal service manager's organization throughout all communications and incident management and resolution activities.

Benefits of Outsourcing

Benefits to engaging with a 3rd-party NOC or Service Desk provider may include:

- The ability to scale services broadly and quickly
- Improve performance metrics
- Utilize highly-skilled and costly internal resources for more profitable tasks and activities

- Increase customer satisfaction through improved, consistent KPIs
- Increase net profits by lowering costs

Considerations Prior to Outsourcing

When exploring outsourcing components of the NOC or Service Desk to a 3rd-party provider, among other concerns, the outsourced service provider or internal services manager may consider:

- The 3rd-party provider's location
- The 3rd-party provider's qualifications and experience
- The 3rd-party provider's business structure and time in business
- The 3rd-party provider's solvency
- The 3rd-party provider's tools and technology and ability to integrate with the provider's existing solutions
- The 3rd-party provider's NOC and Service Desk delivery and management processes
- The 3rd-party provider's training and support offerings
- The 3rd-party provider's customer service philosophy
- The 3rd-party provider's privacy policy
- The 3rd-party provider's culture and native language
- The 3rd-party provider's SLA and KPIs
- The 3rd-party provider's customer satisfaction rating

- The 3rd-party provider's pricing and payment model
- The 3rd-party provider's ability to private label their services and represent themselves as the provider
- The 3rd-party provider's perception in the industry

In addition, the outsourced service provider or internal service manager may request an NDA from the 3rd-party provider prior to negotiating at a deep level where internal and client-specific information may be shared.

What to Outsource

Industry statistics reflect that best in class Service Desks close 90% of service requests with Tier 1 resolution in less than an hour. That means that only 10% of all service requests are escalated to Tier 2 and beyond. Let's assume that 7% of all service requests are escalated to Tier 2, with the remaining 3% ending up in Tier 3.

This means that if the outsourced service provider or internal service manager outsourced their Tier 1 and Tier 2 service requests to a 3rd-party Service Desk, they may potentially reduce their incoming ticket load by up to 97%.

Imagine the potential impact that this has on the ability to repurpose or eliminate internal staff as a result. If highly-skilled, costly internal staff can be reassigned to focus on higher-value, higher-visibility and more profitable services,

---

---

this is a beneficial outcome. And if some costly internal staff can be released, this can also improve net profits.

Outsourcing NOC services to a 3rd-party organization can have similar positive outcomes for the outsourced service provider or internal service manager, and when both Service Desk and NOC services are outsourced to the same 3rd-party provider, this reduces complexity and costs over time, as all NOC and Tier 1 and Tier 2 service delivery activity is conducted by a sole provider. This eases integration, escalation, reporting, communication between, and overall management of the relationship and service outcomes.

The outsourced service provider or internal service manager may outsource:

- Tier 1 and 2 NOC and Service Desk functions

What to Keep
When outsourcing components of the NOC and Service Desk and transferring the role of the single point of contact to a 3rd-party provider, the outsourced service provider or internal service manager would be well advised to monitor and manage the Professional Services Automation solution to insure all service requests are prioritized, assigned and escalated by the 3rd-party provider in adherence with SLAs. The outsourced service provider or internal service manager should also keep all Tier 3 service requests; as these are

---

---

normally the most visible, high-value incidents from a client perspective, allowing the appropriate sensitivity and attention to be directed to these incidents as quickly as possible by the outsourced service provider or internal service manager. In this scenario, all Tier 3 escalations will be assigned to the outsourced service provider's or internal service manager's staff by the 3rd-party provider.

The outsourced service provider or internal service manager will also want to retain management of all vendors supporting their clients or end users and their activity. This again is a highly-visible, high-value activity that requires sensitivity and direct attention.

The outsourced service provider or internal service manager may keep:

- Monitoring and management of the service board/dispatch portal
- Tier 3 escalations
- Vendor management

Integration
The more tightly integrated the 3rd-party NOC and Service Desk provider's systems and solutions are with the outsourced service provider's or internal service manager's, the more efficient and effective service delivery, visibility and reporting will be. Since reporting is so important in terms of KPI

---

management and utilized to reflect service value to end clients by the outsourced service provider or internal service manager, the tighter the integration between these systems, the easier it will be to aggregate the necessary performance data to generate these critical reports.

Transitioning Clients

It will be simpler to on-board new clients or end users to the 3rd-party NOC and Service Desk provider as the single point of contact than it will existing clients and end users. The reason for this is simple – new clients' and end users' expectations can be set appropriately during pre-sales, on-boarding and service turn-up, or go-live to understand and accept the integrated service delivery process. Existing clients and end users; however, are a different story, as they are being asked to accept a change to an unknown experience, and are comfortable with the existing outsourced service provider's or internal service manager's processes, staff and deliverables.

When transitioning existing end users or clients to a 3rd-party provider, it is imperative for the outsourced service provider or internal service manager to reflect a better experience for them to the decision maker. Some points to impress to the client or end user by the outsourced service provider or internal service manager may include:

- The relationship, management and monitoring of all service delivery processes and KPIs will be retained by the outsourced service provider or internal service manager
- Tier 3 escalations will be retained by the outsourced service provider or internal service manager
- Vendor management responsibilities will be retained by the outsourced service provider or internal service manager
- A more consistent service delivery experience will be delivered to the end users or client
- Speedier call response will be delivered to the end users or client
- Increased first call closure will be delivered to the end users or client
- Increased customer satisfaction will be delivered to the end users or client
- The outsourced service provider or internal service manager will be free to focus on more high-value services for end users or clients that help them achieve their business goals

A final consideration for the outsourced service provider or internal service manager to keep in mind when engaging with a 3rd-party provider is that their NOC and Service Desk Managers' roles will shift from managing internal resources to managing external ones, along with the relationship with the 3rd-party provider. This added responsibility will add substantially to the NOC or Service Desk Managers' duties, as it is always challenging to manage an outsourced, geographically displaced group of people. In order to achieve success in this endeavor, the NOC or Service Desk Manager must over-communicate with the 3rd-party provider and their staff, and continuously monitor their PSA solution's service board or management portal to insure the 3rd-party provider's staff is delivering services competently and adhering to SLAs.

A heavy emphasis on customer satisfaction activity is recommended when using a 3rd-party NOC and Service Desk provider, including conducting face-to-face and anonymous electronic surveying, as well as outsourced 3rd-party telephone survey activities.

Section 9: Resources

This section contains resources you may find useful in building, maintaining and maximizing the performance of your NOC and Service Desk.

Remote Monitoring and Management Solutions

Cloud Services Depot
www.cloudservicesdepot.com

Handsfree Networks
www.handsfreenetworks.com

HoundDog
www.hounddogiseasy.com

IT Control Solutions
www.itcontrolsuite.com

Kaseya
www.kaseya.com

LabTech Software
www.labtechsoft.com

Level Platforms
www.levelplatforms.com

N-able
www.n-able.com

Nagios
www.nagios.org

Silverback Technologies (Dell)
www.silverbacktech.com

VirtualAdministrator
www.virtualadministrator.com

Professional Services Automation and Help Desk Solutions

Autotask
www.autotask.com

ConnectWise
www.connectwise.com

Frontrange Solutions
www.frontrange.com

GWI Software
www.gwi.com

Helpstar
www.helpstar.com

NetHelpDesk
www.nethelpdesk.com

Novo Solutions
www.novosolutions.com

Results Software
www.results-software.com

Scriptlogic
www.helpdesksoftware.com

Shockey Monkey
www.shockeymonkey.com

Remote Access and Control Solutions

Bomgar
www.bomgar.com

GoToMyPC
www.gotomypc.com

LogMeIn
www.logmein.com

Remote Helpdesk
www.gidsoftware.com/remotehelpdesk.htm

UltraVNC
www.uvnc.com

3RD-Party NOC And/Or Service Desk Providers

Ingram Micro Seismic
www.ingrammicro.com/seismic

MSPSN Virtual Service Desk
www.mspsn.com

NetEnrich
www.netenrich.com

Service Desk USA
www.servicedeskusa.com

Zenith Infotech
www.zenithinfotech.com

IT and Managed Services Tools

MSP University
www.mspu.us/en/tools

Financial Benchmarking Tools

MSP University
www.mspu.us/en/tools

Service Leadership Inc.
www.service-leadership.com

DISC Profiling Services

MSP University
www.mspu.us/en/services

Blogs

Arlin Sorensen – Heartland Technology Solutions/HTG
http://peerpower.blogspot.com/

Dave Sobel – Evolve Technologies
http://www.evolvetech.com/blog

Eric Ligman – Microsoft
http://blogs.msdn.com/mssmallbiz

Erick Simpson – MSP University
http://www.mspu.us/blog

Joe Panettieri – MSP Mentor
http://www.mspmentor.net/

Josh Hilliker – Intel vPro™ Expert Center
http://communities.intel.com/community/vproexpert

Karl Palachuk – KP Enterprises
http://smallbizthoughts.blogspot.com/

Mark Crall – Charlotte Tech Care Team
http://techcareteam.com

Susan Bradley – The SBS Diva
http://www.sbsdiva.com/

Stuart Crawford – IT Matters
http://www.stuartcrawford.com/

Vlad Mazek – Own Web Now
http://www.vladville.com/

Peer Groups

Heartland Technology Groups
www.htgmembers.com

MSP University
www.mspu.us

Service Leadership, Inc.
www.service-leadership.com

IT and Managed Services Publications

MSP University
www.mspu.us/en/publications

SMB Books
www.smbbooks.com

Section 10: Forms, Tools and Collateral

We've included on the download available at
www.mspu.us/nocbookregistration.htm each and every
form, tool and piece of collateral discussed in this book – and
then some! These include:

- Certified Network Checklist
- Client Information On-Boarding Document
- Managed Services Agreement Example
- I.T. Solutions and Managed Services Proposal Example
- Managed Services Client Welcome Letter
- Incident Management and Resolution Process Example
- Employment ad for a Service Desk engineer
- Employment ad for a NOC Engineer
- Employment ad for a Service Dispatcher
- Employment ad for a Service Manager
- Role description for a Service Manager
- Role description for a Service Dispatcher
- Role description for a CIO
- HR Hiring Checklist for a New Technical Person
- HR Interview Questions for a new Technical Person
- Employment Offer Letter
- Employment Agreement
- Equipment Loan Agreement

- Best Practices Guide for Creating an MSP Agreement
- Best Practices Guide for Creating an Infrastructure Upgrade and Managed Services Proposal
- Best Practices Guide for Infrastructure, Service Desk and NOC Requirements for Managed Services Delivery
- Best Practices Guide for Processes and Procedures Necessary for Managed Services Delivery
- Best Practices Guide forTools Necessary for Managed Services Delivery
- Bonus Webcast - How to Create your MSP Agreement
- Bonus Webcast – How to Prepare an IT Solutions and Managed Services Proposal
- Bonus Webcast – Conducting Effective Site Surveys and Documenting Networks
- Bonus Webcast - Developing an Effective Helpdesk SLA and Escalation Process
- Bonus Webcast – NOC Operations Best Practices
- Bonus Webcast – Service Desk Best Practices
- Bonus Webcast – Service Dispatch Best Practices
- Bonus Webcast – Problem Management Best Practices
- Bonus Webcast – Pricing and Positioning Managed Services

To watch these webcasts, you will need the codec found here: www.gotomeeting.com/codec

---

The following section describes each of these forms, tools and marketing materials in detail, and how to use them.

Certified Network Checklist

A sample certified network checklist to be used as an example when determining infrastructure requirements for service delivery.

Client Information On-Boarding Document

A sample document used to collect required information for client on-boarding.

Managed Services Agreement Example

A sample managed services agreement included for instructional and informational purposes only, and is not recommended, or warranted for use. Always have your attorney or legal team review any and all agreements or documents that you use in your IT practice. Local laws and liabilities can never be fully covered by any type of generic document, including this sample managed services agreement.

I.T. Solutions and Managed Services Proposal Template

A customized, fill-in-the-blanks proposal template for I.T. solutions and managed services.

Managed Services Client Welcome Letter

A letter welcoming a new client to service delivery with instructions on generating service requests.

Incident Management and Resolution Process Example

A basic Service Desk incident management and resolution process documenting best practices for incident handling.

Employment Ad for a Service Desk Engineer

An employment ad designed for a Service Desk engineer.

Employment Ad for a NOC Engineer

An employment ad designed for a NOC engineer.

Employment Ad for a Service Dispatcher

An employment ad designed for a service dispatcher.

Employment Ad for a Service Manager

An employment ad designed for a service manager.

Role Description for Service Manager

Role Description for a Service Dispatcher

Role Description for a CIO

HR Interview Checklist for a New Technical Person

A checklist to utilize when interviewing a new technical hire.

HR Interview Questions for a New Technical Person

A set of questions to use when interviewing a new technical person.

Creating an Effective Managed Services Agreement

A best practices guide focused on creating an effective Managed Services Agreement

Creating an Infrastructure Upgrade and Managed Services Proposal

A best practices guide focused on creating an effective Infrastructure Upgrade and Managed Services Agreement

Infrastructure, Service Desk and NOC Requirements for Managed Services Delivery

A best practices guide focused on Service Desk and NOC requirements for delivery of Managed Services

Best Practices Processes and Procedures Necessary for Managed Services Delivery

A best practices guide focused on delivering Managed Services effectively and efficiently

---

Tools Necessary for Managed Services Delivery

A best practices guide focused on Managed Services tools

Bonus Webcast - How to Create your Managed Services Agreement

Bonus Webcast – How to Prepare an IT Solutions and Managed Services Proposal

Bonus Webcast – Conducting Effective Site Surveys and Documenting Networks

Bonus Webcast - Developing an Effective Helpdesk SLA and Escalation Process

Bonus Webcast – NOC Operations Best Practices

Bonus Webcast – Service Desk Best Practices

Bonus Webcast – Service Dispatch Best Practices

Bonus Webcast – Problem Management Best Practices

Bonus Webcast – Pricing and Positioning Managed Services

Certified Network Checklist

Servers

- ☐ All Servers with Microsoft Operating Systems running Windows Server 2008 or later
- ☐ All Servers with Microsoft Operating Systems have all of the latest Microsoft Service Packs and Critical Updates installed.
- ☐ All Server Software must be Genuine, Licensed and Vendor-Supported
- ☐ The environment must have a currently licensed, up-to-date and Vendor-Supported Server-based Antivirus Solution protecting all Servers, Desktops, Notebooks/Laptops, and Email.

Desktop PC's and Notebooks/Laptops

- ☐ All Desktop PC's and Notebooks/Laptops with Microsoft Operating Systems running Windows 7 or later.
- ☐ All Desktop PC's and Notebooks/Laptops with Microsoft Operating Systems have all of the latest Microsoft Service Packs and Critical Updates installed.
- ☐ All Non-Microsoft PC's and Notebooks/Laptops must meet similar OS-Specific requirements
- ☐ All Desktop PC and Notebook/Laptop Software must be Genuine, Licensed and Vendor-Supported

Certified Network Checklist

Environment

☐ The environment must have a currently licensed, up-to-date and Vendor-Supported Anti-Spam Solution.

☐ The environment must have a currently licensed, up-to-date and Vendor-Supported Anti-Spyware Solution.

☐ The environment must have a currently licensed, Vendor-Supported Server or Network-based Backup Solution.

☐ The environment must have a currently licensed, Vendor-Supported Firewall between the Internal Network and the Internet.

☐ All Wireless data traffic in the environment must be securely encrypted.

☐ The environment must have a T1 or other form of High-Speed Internet Access with Static IP's.

☐ The environment must contain Spare PC(s) per location

Comments:

_____

_____

_____

Client Information On-Boarding Form

Client Info	
Contact Person	
Office Phone	
Cell Phone	
Home Phone	
E-mail Address	
Address	
Domain Name Info	
Domain Name	
Registrar Name	
Domain Created	
Domain Expires	
DNS Servers	
User Account	
Password	
MX Record(s)	

Client Information On-Boarding Form

A Record(s)	
Other	
Misc	

ISP Info	
ISP	
Internet type (DSL/T-1)	
Bandwidth	
Dynamic or Static	
Usable IP Range	
Subnet	
Gateway	
ISP Tech Support Phone Number	
ISP Tech Support E-mail	
User Account	
Password	
Misc	

The Best NOC and Service Desk Operations BOOK EVER!

Client Information On-Boarding Form

Web & E-mail Hosting	
Web Site Hosted on	
Email Hosted on	
User Account	
Password	
Misc	

Server Info	
Make & Model	
Serial Number	
CPU	
RAM	
RAID Configuration	
SCSI	
Battery Backup	
Server Name	
Administrator Account	
Administrator Password	
Domain name	

Client Information On-Boarding Form

Server LAN IP	
Server's OS	
Server's Role	
Hard Disk Size	
Number of hard drives	
Fault Tolerance	

FireWall

Hardware/Software	
Make/ Model	
LAN IP Address	
WAN IP Address	
User Account	
Password	
Remote Management (Enabled/Disabled)	
Ping (on /off)	
VPN(s)	
Open Ports	
NAT'ing Outside/Inside	

The Best NOC and Service Desk Operations BOOK EVER!

Client Information On-Boarding Form

LAN info	
LAN Subnet	
Server's IP	
Gateway	

Anti-Spam	
Anti-Spam Solution	
Version	
User Account	
Password	

Backup	
Backup Software and Version	
Backup Schedule	
Backup Device (Type & Model)	
Number of back up tapes	
Remote Backup/Vendor Name	
User Account	
Password	

The Best NOC and Service Desk Operations BOOK EVER!

Client Information On-Boarding Form

AntiVirus/ Anti-Spyware	
Virus Protection Software	
Version	
User Account	
Password	
Spy Aware Protection Software	
Version	
User Account	
Password	

User Accounts	
User Name	**Password**

Client Information On-Boarding Form

Workstation Inventory				
Computer name	User	CPU	Memory	Hard drive

Client Information On-Boarding Form

Network Inventory		
Device Name	Make & Model	IP Address

Client Information On-Boarding Form

Printers & Peripherals			
Type & Model	**Share Name**	**Physical Location**	**IP address**
Point of Sale			

Software or Hardware	
Vendor	
Version	
Compatibility	

Managed Services Agreement Example

This sample managed service agreement is included for instructional and informational purposes only, and is not recommended, nor warranted for use.

Always have legal counsel review any and all agreements or documents that you utilize in your IT practice, or distribute to your clients prior to doing so.

Local laws and liabilities can never be fully covered by any type of generic document, including this sample managed service agreement.

Managed Services Agreement

10.   Term of Agreement

11.   This Agreement between

_____, herein referred to as Client, and _____,
hereinafter referred to as Service Provider, is effective upon the date signed, shall remain in force for a period of three years, and be reviewed annually to address any necessary adjustments or modifications. Should adjustments or modifications be required that increase the monthly fees paid for the services rendered under this Agreement, these increases will not exceed _____% of the value of the existing monthly fees due under this Agreement. The Service Agreement automatically renews for a subsequent three year term beginning on the day immediately following the end of the Initial Term, unless either party gives the other ninety (90) days prior written notice of its intent not to renew this Agreement.

   d) This Agreement may be terminated by either Party upon ninety (90) days' written notice if the other Party:

      I.   Fails to fulfill in any material respect its

obligations under this Agreement and does not cure such failure within thirty (30) days' of receipt of such written notice.

II.   Breaches any material term or condition of this Agreement and fails to remedy such breach within thirty (30) days' of receipt of such written notice.

III.   Terminates or suspends its business operations, unless it is succeeded by a permitted assignee under this Agreement.

e)   If either party terminates this Agreement, Service Provider will assist Client in the orderly termination of services, including timely transfer of the services to another designated provider. Client agrees to pay Service Provider the actual costs of rendering such assistance.

12.   Fees and Payment Schedule

Fees will be $_____ per month, invoiced to Client on a Monthly basis, and will become due and payable on the first day of each month. Services will be suspended if payment is not received within 5 days following date due. Refer to Appendix B for services covered by the monthly fee under the terms of this Agreement.

It is understood that any and all Services requested by Client that fall outside of the terms of this Agreement will be considered Projects, and will be quoted and billed as separate, individual Services.

13.   Taxes

It is understood that any Federal, State or Local Taxes applicable shall be added to each invoice for services or materials rendered under this Agreement. Client shall pay any such taxes unless a valid exemption certificate is furnished to Service Provider for the state of use.

14.   Coverage

Remote Helpdesk and Vendor Management of Client's IT networks will be provided to the Client by Service Provider through remote means between the hours of 8:00 am – 5:00 pm Monday through Friday, excluding public holidays. Network Monitoring Services will be provided 24/7/365. All services qualifying under these conditions, as well as Services that fall outside this scope will fall under the provisions of Appendix B.

Hardware costs of any kind are not covered under the terms of this Agreement.

Support and Escalation

Service Provider will respond to Client's Trouble Tickets under the provisions of Appendix A, and with best effort after hours or on holidays. Trouble Tickets must be opened by Client's designated I.T. Contact Person, by email to our Help Desk, or by phone if email is unavailable. Each call will be assigned a Trouble Ticket number for tracking. Our escalation process is detailed in Appendix A.

Service outside Normal Working Hours

Emergency services performed outside of the hours of 8:00 am – 5:00 pm Monday through Friday, excluding public holidays, shall be subject to provisions of Appendix B.

Service Calls Where No Trouble is found

If Client requests onsite service and no problem is found or reproduced, Client shall be billed at the current applicable rates as indicated in Appendix B.

Limitation of Liability

In no event shall Service Provider be held liable for indirect, special, incidental or consequential damages arising out of service provided hereunder, including but not limited to loss of profits or revenue, loss of use of equipment, lost data, costs of substitute equipment, or other costs.

15.   Additional Maintenance Services

Hardware/System Support

Service Provider shall provide support of all hardware and systems specified in Appendix B, provided that all Hardware is covered under a currently active Vendor Support Contract; or replaceable parts be readily available, and all Software be Genuine, Currently Licensed and Vendor-Supported. Should any hardware or systems fail to meet these provisions, they will be excluded from this Service Agreement. Should 3rd Party Vendor Support Charges be required in order to resolve any issues, these will be passed on to the Client after first receiving the Client's authorization to incur them.

Virus Recovery for Current, Licensed Antivirus protected systems

Damages caused by, and recovery from, virus infection not detected and quarantined by the latest Antivirus definitions are covered under the terms of this Agreement. This Service is limited to those systems protected with a Currently Licensed, Vendor-Supported Antivirus Solution.

Monitoring Services

Service Provider will provide ongoing monitoring and security services of all critical devices as indicated in Appendix B. Service Provider will provide monthly reports as well as document critical alerts, scans and event resolutions to Client. Should a problem be discovered during monitoring, Service Provider shall make every attempt to rectify the condition in a timely manner through remote means.

16. ### Suitability of Existing Environment
Minimum Standards Required for Services

In order for Client's existing environment to qualify for Service Provider's Managed Services, the following requirements must be met:

Managed Services Agreement Example

---

1. All Servers with Microsoft Windows Operating Systems must be running Windows 2008 Server or later, and have all of the latest Microsoft Service Packs and Critical Updates installed.
2. All Desktop PC's and notebooks/laptops with Microsoft Windows operating systems must be running Windows 7 or later, and have all of the latest Microsoft service packs and critical updates installed.
3. All Server and Desktop Software must be genuine, licensed and vendor-supported.
4. The environment must have a currently licensed, up-to-date and vendor-supported server-based antivirus solution protecting all servers, desktops, notebooks/laptops, and email.
5. The environment must have a currently licensed, vendor-supported server-based backup solution.
6. The environment must have a currently licensed, vendor-supported hardware firewall between the internal network and the Internet.
7. Any Wireless data traffic in the environment must be secured with a minimum of 128bit data encryption.

Costs required to bring Client's environment up to these Minimum Standards are not included in this Agreement.

17.   **Excluded Services**

Service rendered under this Agreement does not include:

11)   Parts, equipment or software not covered by vendor/manufacturer warranty or support.

12)   The cost of any parts, equipment, or shipping charges of any kind.

13)   The cost of any Software, Licensing, or Software Renewal or Upgrade Fees of any kind.

14)   The cost of any 3rd Party Vendor or Manufacturer Support or Incident Fees of any kind.

15)   The cost to bring Client's environment up to minimum standards required for Services.

16)   Failure due to acts of God, building modifications, power failures or other adverse environmental conditions or factors.

17)   Service and repair made necessary by the alteration or modification of equipment other than that authorized by Service Provider,

including alterations, software installations or modifications of equipment made by Client's employees or anyone other than Service Provider.

18) Maintenance of Applications software packages, whether acquired from Service Provider or any other source unless as specified in Appendix B.

19) Programming (modification of software code) and program (software) maintenance unless as specified in Appendix B.

20) Training Services of any kind.

18. Miscellaneous

This Agreement shall be governed by the laws of the State of _____. It constitutes the entire Agreement between Client and Service Provider for monitoring/maintenance/service of all equipment listed in "Appendix B." Its terms and conditions shall prevail should there be any variance with the terms and conditions of any order submitted by Client.

Service Provider is not responsible for failure to render services due to circumstances beyond its control including, but not limited to, acts of God.

---

19. **Acceptance of Service Agreement**

This Service Agreement covers only those services and equipment listed in "Appendix B." Service Provider must deem any equipment/services Client may want to add to this Agreement after the effective date acceptable. The addition of equipment/services not listed in "Appendix B" at the signing of this Agreement, if acceptable to Service Provider, shall result in an adjustment to the Client's monthly charges.

IN WITNESS WHEREOF, the parties hereto have caused this Service Agreement to be signed by their duly authorized representatives as of the date set forth below.

Accepted by:

Authorized Signature   Service Provider   Date

Authorized Signature   Client   Date

Managed Services Agreement

Appendix A

Response and Resolution Times

The following table shows the targets of response and resolution times for each priority level:

Trouble	Priority	Response time (in hours) *	Resolution time (in hours) *	Escalation threshold (in hours)
Service not available (all users and functions unavailable).	1	Within 1 hour	ASAP – Best Effort	2 hours
Significant degradation of service (large number of users or business critical functions affected)	2	Within 4 hours	ASAP – Best Effort	4 hours
Limited degradation of service (limited number of users or functions affected, business process can continue).	3	Within 24 hours	ASAP – Best Effort	48 hours
Small service degradation (business process can continue, one user affected).	4	within 48 hours	ASAP – Best Effort	96 hours

---

Support Tiers

The following details and describes our Support Tier levels:

Support Tier	Description
Tier 1 Support	All support incidents begin in Tier 1, where the initial trouble ticket is created, the issue is identified and clearly documented, and basic hardware/software troubleshooting is initiated.
Tier 2 Support	All support incidents that cannot be resolved with Tier 1 Support are escalated to Tier 2, where more complex support on hardware/software issues can be provided by more experienced Engineers.
Tier 3 Support	Support Incidents that cannot be resolved by Tier 2 Support are escalated to Tier 3, where support is provided by the most qualified and experienced Engineers who have the ability to collaborate with 3rd Party (Vendor) Support Engineers to resolve the most complex issues.

Managed Services Agreement

Appendix A (cont)

Service Request Escalation Procedure

1. Support Request is Received
2. Trouble Ticket is Created
3. Issue is Identified and documented in Help Desk system
4. Issue is qualified to determine if it can be resolved through Tier 1 Support

   If issue can be resolved through Tier 1 Support:

5. Level 1 Resolution - issue is worked to successful resolution
6. Quality Control –Issue is verified to be resolved to Client's satisfaction
7. Trouble Ticket is closed, after complete problem resolution details have been updated in Help Desk system

---

If issue cannot be resolved through Tier 1 Support:

6. Issue is escalated to Tier 2 Support
7. Issue is qualified to determine if it can be resolved by Tier 2 Support

If issue can be resolved through Tier 2 Support:

8. Level 2 Resolution - issue is worked to successful resolution
9. Quality Control —Issue is verified to be resolved to Client's satisfaction
10. Trouble Ticket is closed, after complete problem resolution details have been updated in Help Desk system

If issue cannot be resolved through Tier 2 Support:

9. Issue is escalated to Tier 3 Support
10. Issue is qualified to determine if it can be resolved through Tier 3 Support

---

If issue can be resolved through Tier 3 Support:

11. Level 3 Resolution - issue is worked to successful resolution

12. Quality Control –Issue is verified to be resolved to Client's satisfaction

13. Trouble Ticket is closed, after complete problem resolution details have been updated in Help Desk system

If issue cannot be resolved through Tier 3 Support:

12. Issue is escalated to Onsite Support

13. Issue is qualified to determine if it can be resolved through Onsite Support

If issue can be resolved through Onsite Support:

14. Onsite Resolution - issue is worked to successful resolution

15. Quality Control –Issue is verified to be resolved to Client's satisfaction

---

---

16. Trouble Ticket is closed, after complete problem resolution details have been updated in Help Desk system

    If issue cannot be resolved through Onsite Support:

17. I.T. Manager Decision Point – request is updated with complete details of all activity performed

Managed Services Agreement
Appendix B

Description	Frequency	Included in Maintenance
General		
Document software and hardware changes	As performed	YES
Test backups with restores	Monthly	YES
Monthly reports of work accomplished, work in progress, etc.	Monthly	YES
Systems		
Check print queues	As needed	YES
Ensure that all server services are running	Daily/hourly	YES
Keep Service Packs, Patches and Hotfixes current as per company policy	Monthly	YES
Check event log of every server and identify any potential issues	As things appear	YES
Monitor hard drive free space on server, clients	Daily/hourly	YES
Reboot servers if needed	As needed	YES
Run defrag and chkdsk on all drives	As needed	YES
Scheduled off time server maintenance	As needed	YES
Install software upgrades	As needed	YES
Determine logical directory structure, Implement, MAP, and detail	Revisit Monthly	YES
Set up and maintain groups (accounting, admin, printers, sales, warehouse, etc)	As needed	YES
Check status of backup and restores	Daily	YES
Alert office manager to dangerous conditions -Memory running low -Hard drive showing sign of failure -Hard drive running out of disk space -Controllers losing interrupts -Network Cards report unusual collision activity	As needed	YES
Educate and correct user errors (deleted files, corrupted files, etc.)	As needed	YES
Clean and prune directory structure, keep efficient and active	Monthly	YES
Disaster Recovery		
Disaster Recovery of Server(s)	As Needed	YES

Managed Services Agreement
Appendix B (cont.)

Networks

Check router logs	Weekly	YES
Performance Monitoring/Capacity Planning	Weekly	YES
Monitor DSU/TSU, switches, hubs and internet connectivity, and make sure everything is operational (available for SNMP manageable devices only)	Weekly	YES
Major SW/HW upgrades to network backbone, including routers, WAN additions, etc.	As needed	YES
Maintain office connectivity to the Internet	Ongoing	YES

Security

Check firewall logs	Monthly	YES
Confirm that antivirus virus definition auto updates have occurred	As Needed	YES
Confirm that virus updates have occurred	As Needed	YES
Confirm that backup has been performed on a daily basis	Daily	YES
Create new directories, shares and security groups, new accounts, disable/delete old accounts, manage account policies	As Needed	YES
Permissions and file system management	As Needed	YES
Set up new users including login restrictions, passwords, security, applications	As needed	YES
Set up and change security for users and applications	As needed	YES
Monitor for unusual activity among users	Ongoing	YES

Apps

Exchange user/mailbox management	As needed	YES
Monitor directory replication	As needed	YES
Monitor WINS replication	As needed	YES
SQL server management	As needed	YES
Overall application disk space management	As needed	YES
Ensure Microsoft Office Applications are functioning as designed	As needed	YES

Managed Services Agreement

Appendix B (cont)

Service Rates

Labor	Rate
Remote PC Management/Help Desk 8am-5pm M-F	INCLUDED
Remote Printer Management 8am-5pm M-F	INCLUDED
Remote Network Management 8am-5pm M-F	INCLUDED
Remote Server Management 8am-5pm M-F	INCLUDED
24x7x365 Network Monitoring	INCLUDED
Lab Labor 8am-5pm M-F	INCLUDED
Onsite Labor 8am-5pm M-F	INCLUDED
Remote PC Management/Help Desk 5:01pm-9pm M-F	$____/hr
Remote Printer Management 5:01pm-9pm M-F	$____/hr
Remote Network Management 5:01pm-9pm M-F	$____/hr
Remote Server Management 5:01pm-9pm M-F	$____/hr
Lab Labor 5:01pm-9pm M-F	$____/hr
Onsite Labor 5:01pm-9pm M-F	$____/hr
Remote Labor All Other Times	$____/hr
Lab Labor All Other Times	$____/hr
Onsite Labor All Other Times	$____/hr

Covered Equipment

Managed Desktops: Desktops/Notebooks
Managed Printers:
Managed Networks:
Managed Servers:

I.T. Solutions and Managed Services Proposal Example

Section

1

Review

Introduction

YOUR COMPANY NAME has been providing information technology solutions to the SMB market since YEAR. Our relationships with partners such as Microsoft, Cisco, Citrix, HP, Dell, Veritas and Trend have allowed us the ability to design, scale and implement effective infrastructure solutions for our diverse client base. Our solution stack includes hosted voice over IP services, application and web development, wireless, local and wide-area networking, as well as managed services. As a Gold Certified Microsoft partner, our core competencies include Information Worker Solutions, Networking Infrastructure Solutions, Advanced Infrastructure Solutions, Microsoft Business Solutions, and we are a Microsoft Small Business Specialist.

We specialize in educating you in the information technology options available to ease your business' IT concerns in the 21st century. Our professional scope ranges from engineering and implementing local and wide area networking solutions to architecting and designing custom software applications to address your specific business needs. YOUR COMPANY NAME's network and software applications engineers' combined experience allow us the ability to successfully provide custom, affordable solutions to our valued Clients.

Our technical expertise enables us to provide network design and support, as well as application development for office automation, and Internet/Intranet development and support; utilizing technologies such as digital subscriber line, frame relay, point-to-point tunneling protocol and virtual private networking. These technologies provide the ability to securely encrypt data transmission, paving the way for electronic commerce and e-business.

By coordinating and managing all of your technical solutions and vendors, and proactively managing your network, we allow you the ability to completely focus on running your business.

YOUR COMPANY NAME is uniquely qualified to provide IT project and ongoing service support for YOUR CLIENT NAME. We sincerely appreciate the opportunity to present this proposal.

YOUR COMPANY NAME Bio

Certifications

Microsoft Gold Certified Partner

Microsoft Business Solutions Partner

Microsoft Small Business Specialist

Microsoft Information Worker Competency

Microsoft Networking Infrastructure Competency

Microsoft Advanced Networking Infrastructure Competency

Cisco Partner

Citrix Partner

Partnerships/Affiliations

SMBTN Partner

ASCII Group Member

Vendor Affiliations

Hewlett-Packard Authorized Business Development Partner

Dell Solution Provider Direct

Cisco Reseller

Level Platforms Partner

Zenith Infotech Partner

Symantec/Veritas Partner

ConnectWise Partner

Trend Micro Partner

Initial Site Inspection

General

Physical inspections of YOUR CLIENT NAME'S primary location, and meetings with YOUR CLIENT NAME'S representative(s) were used to compile the results of this proposal. During our initial site inspection, YOUR CLIENT NAME'S local area network, connected client pc's, server(s) and other networked devices were inspected in order to determine their existing configurations and current operating status.

Local Area Network (DESCRIBE YOUR CLIENT'S NETWORK)

YOUR CLIENT NAME'S business operations span between 2 physically displaced buildings, their Main facility and their Irvine Facility. Each of these facilities operates under physically segregated networks, with VPN connectivity to join them. The Main facility's existing local area network is comprised of several 10/100 Network Switches and hubs connected to the new Straitshot DSL router. A Microsoft Windows SBS2003 Server, the client workstations and several network printers and copiers are connected to the inside interface. The IP address on the outside interface of the router is X.X.X.X. DNS Servers being used are X.X.X.X and X.X.X.X. The inside IP address of the router is X.X.X.X. The server is being used as the DHCP server for the network and is Leasing IP addresses in the 192.168.1.x range. The router is

---

forwarding traffic from the outside on ports 80, 3389, 110, and 443 to the inside IP address of the SBS Server, X.X.X.X. The router is also forwarding traffic from the outside on ports 80 and 1494 to the inside IP address of the Citrix server, X.X.X.X. In addition the router is forwarding mail traffic from the outside on port 25 to the inside IP address of the Barracuda server, X.X.X.X.

Additionally, there is a D-Link secure wireless access point in the Main facility's server room.

YOUR CLIENT NAME'S Irvine facility's existing local area network is comprised of two Dell 24 port switches connected to a new CyberGuard SG565 firewall router and the facility's ISP's Cox communication DSL router on the outside interface. The new IRVINE server is being used as a domain controller and DHCP server for the network and is leasing IP addresses in the 192.168.2.x range. The router is forwarding traffic from the outside on port 3389 to the inside IP address of the Irvine server, 192.168.2.230.

YOUR CLIENT NAME'S is subletting space in the Main and Irvine facilities, and is sharing the DSL service in these facilities with the tenants.

YOUR CLIENT NAME'S operates two incompatible phone systems at each of their facilities, with the Main facility phone

---

system comprised of an antiquated server-based PBX. While the Irvine facility has temporary off the shelf analog phones.

Existing LAN Diagram (CREATE A DRAWING)

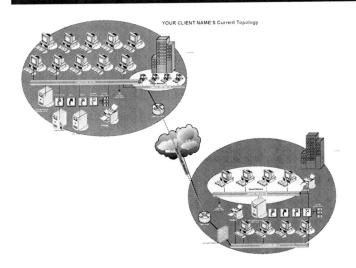

YOUR CLIENT NAME'S Current Topology

I.T. Solutions and Managed Services Proposal Example

Problems at Main and Irvine Facilities (DETAIL AREAS OF CONCERN)

Server

YOUR CLIENT NAME'S new HP Proliant Windows SBS2003 server is configured incorrectly. Upon initial inspection, it was discovered that all of the purpose-built Microsoft Small Business Server tools and wizards have been disabled or ignored. Some of these functions have been manually recreated, contradicting Microsoft's best practices. These purpose-built tools have been specifically designed by Microsoft to properly integrate all the enterprise level features for the operating system. In addition, the domain YOUR CLIENT NAME -Co.com has been improperly named identically to the public YOUR CLIENT NAME'S website domain, www. YOUR CLIENT NAME.com. This can cause name resolution problems and unnecessary network activity, degrading network throughput.

In addition, there are core problems with the server's Internet Information Service (IIS). It was discovered that the server's web component which hosts the company's SharePoint Team Services site, as well as Outlook Web Access and Remote Web Workplace, was not functioning. These features and services are three of the most beneficial attributes of owning Windows Small Business Server 2003. These core components have

---

---

been removed for no conceivable reason, and will need to be recreated for the restoration of proper functionality to the SBS2003 Server.

YOUR CLIENT NAME'S Citrix application server is not operating properly. This has caused the users much anguish and lost productivity, negatively affecting YOUR CLIENT NAME'S bottom line.

Additionally, YOUR CLIENT NAME'S Blackberry server has no security in place.

Workstations

Most of the laptops in Irvine have expired AntiVirus software and no AntiSpyware software installed.

Licensing

It appears the MS Exchange, email server is licensed only for 20 users. On Wednesday the 19th we saw at least 24 users connected. This will ultimately cause email errors and downtime if the server is not properly licensed.

In addition, it appears that the Microsoft Office software on all the Irvine facility laptops may be pirated.

Network Backbone

The network backbone has been neglected. There is a 48 port hub stacked on a 24 port switch. Hubs are essentially less intelligent and slower than switches, while the cost difference is negligible. This may be slowing network traffic at the Main facility. Wireless connectivity is also a concern at both facilities due to the wireless access points being off the shelf home user devices, instead of business-class products.

Lastly, **YOUR CLIENT NAME** is subletting space to tenants in both facilities. Since there is no segregation between the tenant networks and the **YOUR CLIENT NAME** networks, the tenants have may be able to access sensitive **YOUR CLIENT NAME** files and corporate data. In addition, the tenants can tax the Internet bandwidth from Citrix during their normal daily operations, as well as unknowingly infect **YOUR CLIENT NAME'S** network and devices with viruses, spyware and worms.

General (DOCUMENT A GENERAL OVERVIEW OF WORK SCOPE)

Phase 1- **YOUR CLIENT NAME'S** representative(s) indicated the need to remediate their new Windows Small Business Server 2003, which hosts several applications, to allow for a stable, secure computing environment, providing both data and hardware fault-tolerance. The quickest way to help the Irvine office is to clean up the Citrix server errors. We will

---

---

reconfigure the Outlook configuration on the Irvine laptops so they can send and receive mail from any location instead of just the office.

Phase 2- We will upgrade the Citrix server to Windows 2003 Server R2, add 4GB of RAM, and two 200GB hard drives for the DFS synchronization with Irvine.

Additionally, we will correct the wide open security problem on the BlackBerry server. The Irvine laptops will have Symantec AntiVirus and Microsoft AntiSpyware installed on them.

The Blackberry server will be secured.

The tenants network access will be segregated from the YOUR CLIENT NAME network to prevent virus infections or access to YOUR CLIENT NAME data. We will also use the Irvine location's Cyberguard SG565 Firewall to throttle the tenants Internet bandwidth, and in Danville we will move the Tenants to the old SBC Internet circuit. In Danville we will install a new HP Procurve 48 port Switch to replace the aging Hub, and install a CyberGuard SG565 for business class Internet and Wireless access. In Irvine we will use the existing Linksys wireless router for the tenants, and enable the wireless feature on the Cyberguard SG565 router for the YOUR CLIENT NAME Users.

We will purchase and implement 15 new Exchange (SBS) Server licenses and 5 new Microsoft Office Licenses for the laptops.

In addition, the Voice over IP implementation will be completed in Danville in order to provide a solution to the antiquated phone system, and provide the ability to make calls between the Danville and Irvine facilities without incurring Toll charges.

Once these issues have been addressed, we will be able to implement our proactive managed services maintenance plan.

Implementation (DOCUMENT A HIGH-LEVEL PROJECT PLAN)

Approach:

We propose attempting to reconfigure the server by re-running specific portions of the Small Business Server 2003 installation routines. If successful, this will allow the ability to correct the numerous problems detected during our initial inspections. If unsuccessful, we will recommend backing up all of the data on the server, and reinstalling the operating system from scratch. This will be a lengthier and more involved process, and will only be recommended should our initial attempts to repair the server with the first option fail.

We also propose immediately segregating both the Irvine and Danville facilitys' networks from the tenant networks. We recommend purchasing a second Cyberguard SG565 firewall for Danville, to standardize the hardware between both facilities. We also recommend the purchase of an HP Procurve 48 port switch for the Main facility. This switch will improve speed across the network, and allow the best connectivity between facilities.

We will securely encrypt the wireless access points in both facilities, so that only authorized users can utilize these wireless services.

We will redirect both the Irvine and Main users' My Documents folders to their server home folders so that if a workstation dies, the data does not die with it. We will configure the Irvine users' My Documents folders to synchronize between their workstations and the server, in order to eliminate any potential lag time across the VPN. This will allow all users' documents to be backed up by the server. We will configure all users' Outlook applications with Cached Exchange Mode, to further eliminate any lag time across the VPN. Additionally, we will configure RPC over HTTP, allowing the ability for home users to access their email with the full OUTLOOK client, if they so desire.

We also recommend purchasing a spare PC for each
YOUR CLIENT NAME'S location.

Danville server reconfiguration /troubleshooting	*12 Hours*

- **A** YOUR COMPANY NAME'S Representatives
  will spend 12 hours remotely reconfiguring the
  SBS2003 server and Citrix server, as well as
  securing the Blackberry server.

- The goal of this phase is to upgrade the Citrix
  Server to Windows Server 2003 R2 and
  troubleshoot Citrix functionality, remediate
  your Windows SBS2003 Server and correct
  the Active Directory, DNS, IIS and other
  problems with the server, and insure it is
  configured and operating per Microsoft's best
  practices.

Irvine facility network segregation /switch installation /VPN installation & configuration	*8 Hours*

- One YOUR COMPANY NAME'S representative
  will spend 8 hours at YOUR CLIENT NAME'S
  Irvine facility in the network
  segregation/switch/VPN installation phase.

- The goal of this phase is to install the new
  network switches and Cyberguard Firewall
  VPN routers at each of YOUR CLIENT NAME'S

---

buildings and build the VPN tunnel between facilities.

- o The Irvine facility's network will be segregated from the tenant's network by repurposing one of the existing hubs and splitting the DSL circuit behind the two networks.

Secure wireless access point   **2 Hours**

- One YOUR COMPANY NAME'S representative will secure the wireless access points and provide YOUR CLIENT NAME'S representatives the encryption key, and train them on how to create connections.

Redirect all users' home folders to server /configure cached exchange mode   **12 Hours**

- One YOUR COMPANY NAME'S representative will spend 8 hours at YOUR CLIENT NAME'S headquarters redirecting all users' My Documents folders to the server's home folders, and configuring Outlook to operate in Cached Exchange Mode.
- One YOUR COMPANY NAME'S representative will spend 4 hours at the Irvine facility redirecting all users' My Documents folders to the server's home folders, and configuring Outlook to operate in Cached Exchange Mode.

Proposed Redesign (CREATE AN "AFTER" DRAWING)

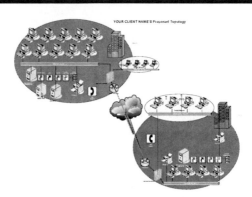

Proposed Managed Services

After the proposed project scope has been completed, YOUR COMPANY NAME will configure YOUR CLIENT NAME'S network and all connected Servers, routers, switches, pc's and peripherals to allow us the ability to proactively manage and maintain your network environment.

The core components that comprise our proactive managed services package include:

- *"All You Can Eat" remote helpdesk during business hours*
- *24x7x365 network and critical device monitoring*
- *Vendor management*

Benefits you will receive as a result of our proactive managed services package include:

- *Much faster response time to trouble tickets*
- *Predictive, proactive IT support*
- *Increased operational efficiency*
- *Reduce and control your operating costs*
- *Cost-effectively gain access to enterprise-level support staff*
- *Experience minimized downtime*
- *Regain the ability to focus on running your business, not your vendors*
- *Receive peace of mind knowing that your network is being monitored 24 Hours a Day, seven days a Week*

Summary (SUMMARIZE THE PROPOSAL AND YOUR QUALIFICATIONS)

YOUR COMPANY NAME has installed, configured and manages over xxx Microsoft Small Business Servers, and maintains Microsoft's *Small Business Specialist Certification*, as well as *Microsoft Gold Certified Partner* status, which is achieved by less than 1% of all Microsoft partners worldwide.

YOUR COMPANY NAME will remediate your Microsoft Windows Small Business Server 2003 and reconfigure it according to Microsoft's best practices. When complete,

---

this will allow the users that you designate the ability to remote directly into their workstations to work, check email remotely, and allow you to maintain your own company Intranet, document management and company calendar.

In addition, we will upgrade your Citrix server to Windows 2003 Server R2 to improve your DFS functionality, as well as securing your Blackberry server. We will segregate and bandwidth-throttle your tenant's networks, and re-purpose the existing wireless access points for their use. We will enable and configure the Cyberguard Firewall routers' wireless capability to provide secure wireless access to designated **YOUR CLIENT NAME'S** Users.

We will also implement a secure VPN solution connecting your two facilities, and configure secure wireless access for your locations. Your users' data will be secure, as we will redirect all of their My Documents folders to the server's home folders for nightly backup. We will also configure Outlook Anti-Spam filtering by configuring Cached Exchange Mode on all workstations.

Once these items have been addressed, we will implement a proactive managed services maintenance plan that will allow you the ability to budget your IT service costs as a flat fee each and every month, saving you costs and downtime, and providing predictive, proactive problem resolution through our all you can eat help desk.

Support:

YOUR COMPANY NAME's Technical Support Center answers service calls 24 hours a day, 7 days a week. Our help desk is staffed with experienced technicians from 7am to 5pm. From 5pm to 7am our answering service contacts an on-call engineer who will return your call and diligently work your problem to a successful resolution. Our managed service agreement clients also benefit from remote support, whereby our technicians utilize remote access tools connecting them to your office systems, allowing the ability to diagnose hardware and software failures via dedicated Internet connections. All of our service agreement clients receive priority service.

Requirements:

YOUR COMPANY NAME's personnel will maintain all documentation. This will include recommendations, schematics, drawings, and configuration data. All work possible will be performed during regular business hours. We will not disrupt normal production by performing server work during these hours.

Locations:

Onsite labor will be performed at YOUR CLIENT NAME'S facilities as required. All remote labor will be performed at YOUR COMPANY NAME'S offices.

Exclusions:

This proposal does not include electrical wiring or panels, network cabling, jacks and related equipment or labor. Other requirements that may be needed, but are not listed in this proposal are deemed outside the scope of this proposal and are therefore not included. Cabling and equipment cannot be quoted until YOUR COMPANY NAME is provided with a scope of work.

Installation Dates:

To be determined.

Sample Managed Services Welcome Letter

Congratulations and Welcome to (Your Company Name) – the Premier Managed I.T. Solution Provider.

Since (Inception Date), (Your Company Name) has been developing and implementing Information Technology Solutions that improve our Clients' Business Processes, adding value to their Bottom Line.

Our new *Managed Services Plan* is a direct result of our continual effort to identify our Clients' needs, and alleviate their business pain.

We are pleased and excited to introduce this valuable Service to you and your Organization. We are now your I.T. Department, and will provide Technical Support for each User and Device on your Network, as detailed in your Managed Services Agreement.

Your Managed Services Plan provides you with *Unlimited Help Desk/Remote Support* during the hours of 8am and 5pm Monday through Friday, excluding Holidays. Should your Support need fall outside of these hours; you will be billed as indicated in Appendix "B" of your Managed Services Agreement.

In addition to providing you with Unlimited Help Desk/Remote Support, we will also monitor your Servers and their Critical Services such as Exchange, SQL Databases, and other specific Line-Of-Business Applications installed on them, along with your Internet Connection and Firewall/Routers 24 hours a day, 7 days a week.

Should any of these Services fail, our Network Monitoring Systems will attempt to restart them. Should these attempts fail, a Trouble Ticket will be created immediately, and an Engineer will be alerted to begin troubleshooting. Our goal is to minimize your downtime, and this is just one tool that we rely on to achieve this objective.

We've made it simple to request Support – just send an Email to:

(Your Helpdesk Email Address)

Or, just ask for the Help Desk at (Your Helpdesk Phone Number).

If calling after hours with an Emergency, please dial extension (Your After-Hours Extension), and an On-Call Engineer will be paged immediately.

Vendor Management is also included in your Managed Services Plan. We relieve you of the burden of having to

---

Sample Managed Services Welcome Letter

---

manage all of your Vendors, and allow you the ability to focus on running your business.

You will be contacted shortly by a Customer Service Representative who will gather the information we will need in order to begin providing this valuable Service to you, and to schedule a visit from our Technical Team so that we can begin configuring your Network for Managed Services.

Thank you again for allowing us the opportunity to earn your business. In a short time, I'm sure you'll agree that you're adding tremendous value to your Organization through our Managed Services.

Sincerely,

Incident Management and Resolution Process Example

1. Support Request is Received

2. Trouble Ticket is Created

3. Issue is Identified and documented in Help Desk system

4. Issue is qualified to determine if it can be resolved through Tier 1 Support

   If issue can be resolved through Tier 1 Support:

5. Level 1 Resolution - issue is worked to successful resolution

6. Quality Control –Issue is verified to be resolved to Client's satisfaction

7. Trouble Ticket is closed, after complete problem resolution details have been updated in Help Desk system

---

If issue cannot be resolved through Tier 1 Support:

6. Issue is escalated to Tier 2 Support

7. Issue is qualified to determine if it can be resolved by Tier 2 Support

If issue can be resolved through Tier 2 Support:

8. Level 2 Resolution - issue is worked to successful resolution

9. Quality Control –Issue is verified to be resolved to Client's satisfaction

10. Trouble Ticket is closed, after complete problem resolution details have been updated in Help Desk system

If issue cannot be resolved through Tier 2 Support:

9. Issue is escalated to Tier 3 Support

10. Issue is qualified to determine if it can be resolved through Tier 3 Support

---

If issue can be resolved through Tier 3 Support:

11. Level 3 Resolution - issue is worked to successful resolution
12. Quality Control –Issue is verified to be resolved to Client's satisfaction
13. Trouble Ticket is closed, after complete problem resolution details have been updated in Help Desk system

If issue cannot be resolved through Tier 3 Support:

12. Issue is escalated to Onsite Support
13. Issue is qualified to determine if it can be resolved through Onsite Support

If issue can be resolved through Onsite Support:

14. Onsite Resolution - issue is worked to successful resolution
15. Quality Control –Issue is verified to be resolved to Client's satisfaction

---

16. Trouble Ticket is closed, after complete problem resolution details have been updated in Help Desk system

    If issue cannot be resolved through Onsite Support:

17. I.T. Manager Decision Point – request is updated with complete details of all activity performed

Employment Ad for a Service Desk Engineer

Service Desk Engineer

Company: MSP University
Location: Garden Grove, CA 92841
Status: Full-Time, Employee
Job Category: Service Desk
Relevant Work Experience: 3-5 Years
Career Level: Experienced (Non-Manager)

We are currently seeking a highly skilled Service Desk engineer with the drive and determination to help us support our client base. This position reports to our Service Manager. We are looking for an individual who is a problem-solver and has a proven track record of working within a team environment to successfully address challenging user computing issues, and is accustomed to leveraging technical training opportunities to improve their skills. If you have the experience and the desire, we'd like to talk to you.

Our Service Desk engineers are responsible for maintaining user uptime and improving their computing experiences through effective remote monitoring, maintenance and problem identification and resolution activities, as well as growing and developing the organization's perception with existing clients through exceptional customer service. Candidates must be energetic and focused with a strong motivation to learn new technologies and management and maintenance processes. This position requires dedication, persistence, follow-up, effective utilization of provided resources and unbeatable customer service.

This position will include identifying user problems and working within a structured problem management and resolution process to remediate them within established SLAs, and involves working with other resources and vendors to deliver effective support services. Responsibilities include identifying, documenting and troubleshooting user computing issues to resolution and maintaining client satisfaction.

Job duties include utilizing our remote monitoring and management (RMM) and professional services automation (PSA) solutions along with other service-specific tools and technologies to deliver remote user support services and update service request information, answer technical support calls, assign ticket severity, prioritize work accordingly, and collaborate and work with other staff and vendor support resources to resolve issues. Overall relationship management and the ability to coordinate required resources to respond to complex IT requirements are desired. Other requirements include participating in ongoing training and attainment of manufacturer certifications, developing and maintaining relationships with user and vendor contacts, and preparing and presenting service and monitoring reports to management regularly.

Minimum Skills Required:

- Minimum three years Service Desk experience
- Microsoft Certified Professional status
- Excellent knowledge of our supported software and technologies
- Strong interpersonal skills required to effectively communicate with users and vendors
- Passion for teamwork, continuing education, problem solving and exceptional customer service
- Must be well spoken, outgoing, organized, detailed-orientated, dependable and flexible
- Experience with HP, Cisco and Citrix technologies a plus
- Valid driver's license and proof of insurance
- Background check and drug screen required
- Reliable transportation

This Position Entails:

- Troubleshooting user problems over the phone and with remote control technologies
- Accurate documentation of all activities conducted

- The ability to manage, maintain, troubleshoot and support our users' networks, equipment, software and services
- The ability to learn quickly and adapt to changing requirements

The Successful Candidate must be:

- Professional and articulate
- Interpersonally adept
- Technically proficient
- A relationship builder
- A problem solver

Benefits include group medical/dental insurance, paid vacation, holidays, personal & sick time and training reimbursement. Our generous compensation plans are structured as salary plus bonuses for meeting utilization, compliance and customer service requirements, with initial compensation commensurate with relevant experience.

Qualified candidates please submit a current resume, along with salary history to: hr@mspu.us.

Employment Ad for a NOC Engineer

Network Operations Center (NOC) Engineer

Company: MSP University
Location: Garden Grove, CA 92841
Status: Full-Time, Employee
Job Category: Network Operations
Relevant Work Experience: 3-5 Years
Career Level: Experienced (Non-Manager)

We are currently seeking a highly skilled NOC engineer with the drive and determination to help us support our client base. This position reports to our Service Manager. We are looking for an individual who is a problem-solver and has a proven track record of working within a team environment to successfully address challenging network computing issues, and is accustomed to leveraging technical training opportunities to improve their skills. If you have the experience and the desire, we'd like to talk to you.

Our NOC engineers are responsible for maintaining user uptime and improving their computing experiences through proactive remote monitoring, maintenance and problem identification and resolution activities, as well as growing and developing the organization's perception with existing clients

---

---

through exceptional customer service. Candidates must be energetic and focused with a strong motivation to learn new technologies and management and maintenance processes. This position requires dedication, persistence, follow-up, effective utilization of provided resources and unbeatable customer service.

This position will include identifying hardware, network and service problems and working within a structured problem management and resolution process to remediate them within established SLAs, and involves working with other resources and vendors to deliver effective support services. Responsibilities include identifying, documenting and troubleshooting client network and computing issues to resolution and maintaining client satisfaction.

Job duties include utilizing our remote monitoring and management (RMM) and professional services automation (PSA) solutions along with other service-specific tools and technologies to deliver remote network environment support services and update service request information, answer technical support calls, assign ticket severity, prioritize work accordingly, and collaborate and work with other staff and vendor support resources to resolve issues. Overall relationship management and the ability to coordinate required resources to respond to complex IT requirements are desired. Other requirements include participating in ongoing

---

training and attainment of manufacturer certifications, developing and maintaining relationships with user and vendor contacts, and preparing and presenting service and monitoring reports to management regularly.

Minimum Skills Required:

- Minimum three years NOC experience
- Microsoft Certified Professional status
- Excellent knowledge of our supported software and technologies
- Strong interpersonal skills required to effectively communicate with users and vendors
- Passion for teamwork, continuing education, problem solving and exceptional customer service
- Must be well spoken, outgoing, organized, detailed-orientated, dependable and flexible
- Experience with HP, Cisco and Citrix technologies a plus
- Valid driver's license and proof of insurance
- Background check and drug screen required
- Reliable transportation

This Position Entails:

- Troubleshooting network, equipment and service-related problems with remote control technologies
- Analyzing remote monitoring reports to identify capacity and performance issues and remediate them

---

The Best NOC and Service Desk Operations BOOK EVER!

Employment Ad for a NOC Engineer

- Accurate documentation of all activities conducted
- The ability to manage, maintain, troubleshoot and support our users' networks, equipment, software and services
- The ability to learn quickly and adapt to changing requirements

The Successful Candidate must be:

- Professional and articulate
- Interpersonally adept
- Technically proficient
- A relationship builder
- A problem solver

Benefits include group medical/dental insurance, paid vacation, holidays, personal & sick time and training reimbursement. Our generous compensation plans are structured as salary plus bonuses for meeting utilization, compliance and customer service requirements, with initial compensation commensurate with relevant experience.

Qualified candidates please submit a current resume, along with salary history to: hr@mspu.us.

Employment Ad for a Service Dispatcher

Service Dispatcher

Company: MSP University
Location: Garden Grove, CA 92841
Status: Full-Time, Employee
Job Category: Dispatcher
Relevant Work Experience: 3-5 Years
Career Level: Experienced (Non-Manager)

We are currently seeking a highly skilled service dispatcher with the drive and determination to help us support our client base. This position reports to our Service Manager. We are looking for an individual who is a problem-solver and has a proven track record of working within a team environment to successfully address remote user issues requiring onsite dispatch. If you have the experience and the desire, we'd like to talk to you.

Our service dispatchers participate in our problem management and resolution process, and assign resources to and schedule all remote, onsite or bench services, as well as growing and developing the organization's perception with existing clients through exceptional customer service. Candidates must be energetic and focused with a strong

---

motivation to learn new technologies and management and scheduling processes. This position requires dedication, persistence, follow-up, effective utilization of provided resources and unbeatable customer service.

This position will include coordinating efficient and timely client installation and repair assignments through effective management of our field engineering staff and working within a structured problem management and resolution process to complete them within established SLAs, and involves working with other resources and vendors to deliver effective support services. Responsibilities include continuously monitoring and adjusting work assignments to insure optimum tech productivity through efficient routing and maintaining client satisfaction.

Job duties include utilizing our professional services automation (PSA) solution to monitor remote user support services and update service request information, answer technical support calls, assign ticket severity, prioritize and schedule work accordingly, and collaborate and work with other staff and vendor support resources to resolve issues. Overall relationship management skills and the ability to coordinate required resources to respond to complex IT requirements are desired. Other requirements include participating in ongoing training and preparing and presenting service reports to management regularly.

Employment Ad for a Service Dispatcher

Minimum Skills Required:

- Minimum three years service dispatch experience
- Excellent knowledge of our supported software and technologies
- Strong interpersonal skills required to effectively communicate with users, staff and vendors
- Passion for teamwork, continuing education, problem solving and exceptional customer service
- Must be well spoken, outgoing, organized, detailed-orientated, dependable and flexible
- Valid driver's license and proof of insurance
- Background check and drug screen required
- Reliable transportation

This Position Entails:

- Heavy scheduling and management of human resources
- Efficient and effective routing of each day's scheduled work to the appropriate field engineer
- Accurate documentation of all activities conducted
- Heavy follow-up and follow-through
- The ability to learn quickly and adapt to changing requirements

Employment Ad for a Service Dispatcher

The Successful Candidate must be:

- Professional and articulate
- Interpersonally adept
- Technically proficient
- A relationship builder
- A problem solver

Benefits include group medical/dental insurance, paid vacation, holidays, personal & sick time and training reimbursement. Our generous compensation plans are structured as salary plus bonuses for meeting utilization, compliance and customer service requirements, with initial compensation commensurate with relevant experience.

Qualified candidates please submit a current resume, along with salary history to: hr@mspu.us.

Employment Ad for a Service Manager

Service Manager

Company: MSP University
Location: Garden Grove, CA 92841
Status: Full-Time, Employee
Job Category: Service Management
Relevant Work Experience: 5-7 Years
Career Level: Experienced (Manager)

We are currently seeking a highly skilled service manager with the drive and determination to help us support our client base. This position reports to our Director of Technical Services. We are looking for an individual who is a problem-solver and has a proven track record of managing a technical team to successfully address challenging user computing issues, and is accustomed to maintaining technical staffing levels, training and certification requirements, problem management and resolution processes and client satisfaction via strict SLA management. If you have the experience and the desire, we'd like to talk to you.

Our service manager is responsible for maintaining client uptime and improving their computing experiences through managing our technical staff's effective remote monitoring,

---

maintenance and problem identification and resolution activities, as well as growing and developing the organization's perception with existing clients through exceptional customer service. This position will directly supervise our Service Desk and staff, provide customer service support, analyze trends in client inquiries/requests for assistance, recommend improvements in overall service levels and monitor staff performance. Candidates must be energetic and focused with a strong motivation to learn new technologies and management and maintenance processes. This position requires dedication, persistence, follow-up, effective utilization of provided resources and unbeatable customer service.

This position will include managing a structured problem management and resolution process to remediate client problems within established SLAs, and involves working with other resources and vendors to deliver effective support services.

Job duties include utilizing our professional services automation (PSA) solution to manage technical support services and collaborate and work with other management, staff and vendor support resources to insure effective, efficient service delivery to clients. Overall relationship management skills and the ability to coordinate required resources to respond to complex IT requirements are desired.

Employment Ad for a Service Manager

Other requirements include participating in ongoing management and strategy meetings and preparing and presenting service reports to management regularly.

Minimum Skills Required:

- Minimum three years service dispatch experience
- Excellent knowledge of our supported software and technologies
- Strong interpersonal skills required to effectively communicate with clients, staff and vendors
- Passion for teamwork, problem solving and exceptional customer service
- Must be well spoken, outgoing, organized, detailed-orientated, dependable and flexible
- Valid driver's license and proof of insurance
- Background check and drug screen required
- Reliable transportation

This Position Entails:

- Management of human resources to meet organizational goals for service excellence
- Administrator of established company policies
- Analysis of service delivery business unit data to seek improvements in efficiency and productivity
- Heavy follow-up and follow-through
- The ability to learn quickly and adapt to changing requirements

The Best NOC and Service Desk Operations BOOK EVER!

Employment Ad for a Service Manager

The Successful Candidate must be:

- Professional and articulate
- Interpersonally adept
- Technically proficient
- A relationship builder
- A problem solver

Benefits include group medical/dental insurance, paid vacation, holidays, personal & sick time and training reimbursement. Our generous compensation plans are structured as salary plus bonuses for meeting utilization, compliance and customer service requirements, with initial compensation commensurate with relevant experience.

Qualified candidates please submit a current resume, along with salary history to: hr@mspu.us.

HR Hiring Checklist for a New Technical Person

1.	Run ad for technical person	Completed
2.	Receive and review resume	
3.	Conduct telephone interview	
	• Use standard interview questions	
4.	Email candidate DISC behavioral profile link	
5.	Email candidate PTSI profile link	
	• Email candidate results of profiles before live interview	
6.	Schedule live interview in office	
	• Complete job application and typing test	
	• Review DISC behavioral profile	
	• Review PTSI profile	
	• Give candidate technical test	
	• Review position requirements	
	• Review training process and timeline	
7.	Schedule second interview with upper management	
8.	Establish start date for candidate (at least 1 week out to check references)	
9.	Email offer letter to candidate	
10.	Conduct criminal background check and reference check	
11.	Schedule appointment for drug screen	
12.	New hire orientation	
	• Issue employee handbook	
	• Schedule company training	
	• Company tour and introduction to staff	

HR Interview Questions for a New Technical Person

Primary Questions*

- What do you know about our company?
  What we are looking for is do they know us or have they at least looked at the web site. (we fill them in if they don't know)
- Tell me a little bit about yourself. If needed clarify (tell me about your previous jobs)
- What are some of your strengths ..... Weaknesses?
- What do you see yourself doing in 3 years? .... how about in 5 years?
- Tell me a time when you made a mistake and what steps did you take to resolve the issue?
- What do you get excited about? .... What upsets you?
- What situations make you lose your temper?
- What was one of your greatest successes?
- What are 3 things you do extremely well?
- What are 3 things you need to work on?
- In a group or team what position do you take on?
- Tell us about a team you have worked in.
- What are three positive things your last boss would say about you?
- How much guidance and management do you like?
- How much do you feel you need?
- What type of people do you work best with?

- If budgets were of no concern, what would be the first thing you would spend money on and why?
- What are your compensation requirements?
- Can we have references?
- Can you send us an example of something you've written?
- Do you have any questions for us?

Additional Questions*

- Is there anything that would interfere with your regular attendance?
- What would your perfect job look like?
- Why should we hire you?
- What makes you more qualified than the other applicants?
- What are the skills that you think would benefit our company?
- How do you see yourself fitting in to our organization?
- Rate yourself on a scale of 1-10 on Word, Excel, PowerPoint, Outlook and Vista
- What type of work environment do you like?
- How do you work under pressures & deadlines?
- If you could start your career again, what would you do differently?
- How would you describe your personality? What is your favorite movie of all time? Why?
- Describe a time when you made a client/client extremely happy?

- Do you mind if we call your former employer?
- Why are you considering a career change at this time or leaving your current position?
- What do you like and dislike about your current position?
- What about this position do you find the most attractive? .... Least attractive?
- In your present position, what problems have you identified that had previously been overlooked?
- What kind of feedback have you received from past clients and clients?
- How have you handled negative feedback from clients, clients, or team members?
- Give us an example of a time where there was a conflict in a team/group that you were involved in and how it was resolved.

Information Systems Questions*

- Describe your documentation skills
- Rate yourself on a scale of 1-10 on Windows Vista, Windows 2003 Server, Backup Exec, Visio, Trend/Norton AV.
- How comfortable are you working with various hardware?
- What important trends do you see in our industry?
- Do you hold any certifications?
- How do you feel about attaining certifications?
- Do you own a car and have a driver's license?

The Best NOC and Service Desk Operations BOOK EVER!

HR Interview Questions for a New Technical Person

- Do you mind using your personal vehicle for work?
- What are your hours of availability?
- How do you feel about working some nights and weekends?
- What are the seven layers of the OSI model?
- What sort of cabling is suitable for Fast Ethernet protocols?
- What is the difference between a hub, switch, and router?
- What is a default route?
- What is the difference between TCP and UDP?
- How would you optimize Exchange 2003 memory usage on a Windows Server 2003 server with more than 1Gb of memory?
- What are the standard port numbers for SMTP, POP3, IMAP4, RPC, LDAP and Global Catalog?
- What are the IP address ranges for class A-E? 5.
- What items of information would you request from a user to effectively address a technical problem?
- What command do you use to force the client to give up the DHCP lease if you have access to the client PC?
- What's the difference between forward lookup and reverse lookup zones in DNS?
- How do you breakup a broadcast domain?
- If you were setting up a new PC for an existing user with and existing a PC what steps would you go through?
- What are Levels of RAID 0, 1, 5? Which one is better & why?

- Name key files or directories on a Windows system that should always be backed up.
- What are some things to troubleshoot for an I/O error reported in your backup logs?

Scenario Questions*

- A call comes in to the help desk from a user stating that no one in his or her building can get logged on. The PCs in that building are plugged into a switch and then connected to your building with routers over a T-1 line. What do you do?
- Fifty new PCs are to arrive within two weeks, and you're tasked with installing them. You have a staff of five people. Describe how you would take this project from beginning to end.
- A call comes in from a client that is irate because it has been 3 hours and his/her problem hasn't been fixed yet. Describe how you would deal with this situation step by step.
- What is DHCP and how does it work? What is it used for?
- What is DNS and how does it work? What is it used for?
- Describe what a netmask is. How does it work?

Special thanks to Kurt Sippel from Applied Tech Solutions

MSP University

MSP University specializes in providing managed services training, workshops, and boot camps, as well as sales and marketing services to IT service providers, vendors and channel organizations worldwide through our online Managed Services Provider University at www.mspu.us.

MSP University is a comprehensive, vendor-neutral resource whose sole function is to collect and disseminate as much information as possible and mentor its partners on building, operating and growing a successful I.T. and managed services practice.

Our Mission: To deliver the finest managed services training and support resources available to IT professionals anywhere.

Our Vision: To be recognized as the premier authority on the development and growth of a successful IT managed services practice.

Our Values: Committed to the highest standards of integrity, we fulfill our responsibilities to our partners, our staff and their families in an ethical and professional manner.

What you get: A continuing curriculum dedicated to what every IT service provider needs to know about managed services!

Benefits:

- Access to hundreds of Webinars, teleseminars and forms, tools and collateral – *the most MSP content available anywhere*
- Nearly 600 individual MSP Courses and growing!
- Study and participate in these valuable MSP courses at your own speed
- Unlimited email support
- Participation in live "state of the industry" calls every month

Ask about our MSP Boot Camps:

- 3-Day MSP sales & marketing boot camps
- 2-Day MSP annuity-based solution stack boot camps
- 1-Day NOC/help desk boot camps

What is Managed Services University?

MSP University is the answer for all IT service providers either preparing to transition to an annuity-based managed services delivery model, or who are already delivering managed services, and wish to increase their knowledge of managed

---

services vendors, services, solutions and business, technical and sales and marketing best practices.

Why Managed Services University?

The founders of Managed Services University wished to create a single, comprehensive resource to collect and disseminate as much information as possible about building, operating and growing a successful managed services practice.

What are your qualifications to operate Managed Services University?

We are a subsidiary of Intelligent Enterprise, a Gold Certified Microsoft partner and operators of a successful IT Services Practice since 1997, one of the first "pure-play" MSPs in the SMB space who successfully transitioned to a completely managed services delivery model in January of 2005, and developed and "all you can eat" managed services approach focused on 3 core deliverables – remote help desk, proactive network monitoring and we pioneered vendor management.

Through the creation of a managed services sales and marketing approach unique to the industry, Intelligent Enterprise sold well over $2MM worth of managed services agreements before being asked to share their managed services knowledge and expertise with thousands of I.T.

---

service providers and channel organizations worldwide through our MSP University at www.mspu.us.

In addition to real-world experience, our authorship of "The Guide to a Successful Managed Services Practice – *What Every SMB IT Service Provider Should Know...*", "The Best I.T. Sales & Marketing BOOK EVER!", "The Best NOC and Service Desk Operations BOOK EVER!", and contributions to numerous publications including Microsoft's Expert Column; as well as a series of Microsoft TS2, Cisco and Intel Webcasts and live, in-the-field events with these clients featuring our managed services methodologies, more than qualify us as experts in the field of I.T. solutions and managed services.

What can I expect after joining?

You will gain unlimited access to our hundreds of live and recorded webinars and teleseminars, as well as live regional 1-day workshops, to guide you - no matter where you are on the path to managed services. In addition you will receive unlimited email support from our experienced staff, as well as participation in live group "state of the industry" calls each month to help answer all of your managed services questions.

What types of Courses do you offer?

Unlike other vendor-specific managed services Training offerings, our university curriculum has been consciously

---

designed in a completely agnostic and vendor-neutral manner, allowing us the ability to provide training courses from all MSP vendors who wish to participate, giving you the best opportunity to experience each solution or service to compare head-to-head at your own pace.

In addition to providing access to MSP vendor solutions and services, our courses are a holistic answer to all facets of operating a successful managed services practice, and include:

- Managed Services Concepts
- MSP Vendor Management
- MSP HR Training
- MSP Marketing Process
- MSP Lead Generation
- MSP Sales Process
- MSP Appointment Setting
- MSP Sales Closing Techniques
- MSP Help Desk Best Practices
- MSP Tools
- MSP Service Contracts
- MSP Staffing
- MSP Vendor Solution Partnering
- MSP Additional Annuity-Based Solutions

And more...this is an extremely small sampling of our Courses...

How are University Courses Conducted?

All of our managed services courses, whether they highlight a specific process such as sales and marketing or system monitoring best practices; or spotlight a managed services solution or vendor, are delivered through webinars and teleseminars, which are recorded for offline access.

We also offer regional live workshops and boot camps that deep-dive into specific advanced managed services concepts, as well as one-on-one onsite consulting services.

What other benefits will I receive?

As a MSP University member, in addition to access to all of our live and recorded courses, regional workshops, and email and group call support, you will also receive discounts for all of our boot camp training sessions, and other special offers available only to MSPU members.

How long does MSP University take?

It's completely up to you - our MSP University is a self-paced program delivered through webinars, teleseminars and all-day workshops. It's completely up to you to determine how long it will take to meet your specific needs. Since we are continually adding new content to our university as the managed services industry matures and develops, you may wish to maintain your membership indefinitely.

Do you offer any other Partner Services?

In addition to MSP University, we also provide an economical Managed Marketing Service for our Partners, which handle lead-generation activities for new business in a scheduled, consistent manner.

Our Marketing Department sources Marketing Lists, designs and produces marketing collateral such as your website, letters, postcards and emails, performs the posting and mailing and sets appointments for our partners – allowing them the ability to do what they do best - deliver their services.

We also offer affordable marketing collateral creation services – for those partners who can handle the actual marketing duties themselves, but need help in creating eye-catching collateral, including their website, case studies, white papers, newsletters, line cards, postcards, and developing their marketing message.

How much is Tuition for MSPU?

That's the best part – we have a membership level to meet your specific needs – from a FREE Basic Membership to monthly subscriptions providing unlimited access to our entire managed services curriculum of hundreds of courses (and growing every day!), forms, tools and collateral and FREE

---

attendance to any and all of our Live regional workshops, and email and group call support.

Sounds great! How do I join MSPU?

Simply visit our website at www.mspu.us/join and navigate to the "Registration" tab!

If you're not ready to subscribe to our Premium membership, register for a FREE Basic membership to MSP University, which will provide you with access to all of our Non-Premium content including webinars, tools, forms and collateral. Should you wish to access our Premium content at any time, it's easy to upgrade your membership at any time by visiting http://www.mspu.us/upgrade, providing you the following additional benefits:

- Free Audio Book Download of "The Guide to a Successful Managed Services Practice"
- Free Audio Book Download of "The Best I.T. Sales & Marketing BOOK EVER!"
- Unlimited access to MSPU Premium website training content, updated regularly
- Email support
- Deep discounts on all MSPU products and services
  - Other special offers available only to MSPU Premium Members!

...and much, much more!

What's on the Download?

We've included on the download available at www.mspu.us/nocbookregistration each and every form, tool and piece of collateral discussed in this book – and then some! These include:

- Certified Network Checklist
- Client Information Document
- Managed Services Agreement Example
- I.T. Solutions and Managed Services Proposal Example
- Managed Services Client Welcome Letter
- Incident Management and Resolution Process Example
- Employment ad for a Service Desk engineer
- Employment ad for a NOC Engineer
- Employment ad for a Service Dispatcher
- Employment ad for a Service Manager
- Role description for a Service Manager
- Role description for a Service Dispatcher
- Role description for a CIO
- HR Hiring Checklist for a New Technical Person
- HR Interview Questions for a new Technical Person
- Employment Offer Letter
- Employment Agreement
- Equipment Loan Agreement
- Best Practices Guide for Creating an MSP Agreement
- Best Practices Guide for Creating an Infrastructure Upgrade and Managed Services Proposal

The Best NOC and Service Desk Operations BOOK EVER!

What's on the Download?

- Best Practices Guide for Infrastructure, Service Desk and NOC Requirements for Managed Services Delivery
- Best Practices Guide for Processes and Procedures Necessary for Managed Services Delivery
- Best Practices Guide forTools Necessary for Managed Services Delivery
- Bonus Webcast - How to Create your MSP Agreement
- Bonus Webcast – How to Prepare an IT Solutions and Managed Services Proposal
- Bonus Webcast – Conducting Effective Site Surveys and Documenting Networks
- Bonus Webcast - Developing an Effective Helpdesk SLA and Escalation Process
- Bonus Webcast – NOC Operations Best Practices
- Bonus Webcast – Service Desk Best Practices
- Bonus Webcast – Service Dispatch Best Practices
- Bonus Webcast – Problem Management Best Practices
- Bonus Webcast – Pricing and Positioning Managed Services

To watch these webcasts, you will need the codec found here:

www.gotomeeting.com/codec

Don't forget to register your copy of The Best NOC and Service Desk Operations BOOK EVER! at _www.mspu.us/nocbookregistration_ to receive your downloadable forms, tools and collateral, as well as exclusive additional resources and valuable webinar training absolutely FREE!

CPSIA information can be obtained at www.ICGtesting.com
Printed in the USA
BVOW032241170313

315695BV00009B/143/P